VERGE 2014

VERGE 2014
EVERYTHING AND NOTHING

EDITED BY

GABRIEL GARCIA OCHOA

REBECCA JONES

OSCAR SCHWARTZ

MONASH University
Publishing

Monash University Publishing
Building 4, Monash University
Clayton, Victoria 3800, Australia

www.publishing.monash.edu

Monash University Publishing brings to the world publications which advance the best traditions of humane and enlightened thought.

Monash University Publishing titles pass through a rigorous process of independent peer review.

ISBN: 978-1-922235-49-7

www.publishing.monash.edu/books/verge2014-9781922235497.html

Series: Verge

Design: Les Thomas

Cover image: David Abraham Michael

Printed in Australia by Griffin Press an Accredited ISO AS/NZS 14001:2004 Environmental Management System printer.

The paper this book is printed on is certified against the Forest Stewardship Council ® Standards. Griffin Press holds FSC chain of custody certification SGS-COC-005088. FSC promotes environmentally responsible, socially beneficial and economically viable management of the world's forests.

Contents

Foreword

Gabriel Garcia Ochoa

Why, I wonder, are you reading this Foreword, when you could already be poring through what comes after it, which is to say, the good stuff?

By now you could have singed your fingertips with Peter Dawncy's prose, fiery as its subject matter; you could have lost yourself in the Menippean maze Nick Modrzewski has built for us, trying to find your way out, wondering if Petronius' ghost hides behind those walls of topiary. And yet, here you are ... You are not exploring the secrets of 'The City of Jasmine', a Jewish and post-Jewish Damascus of melancholy beauty dissected by Maria Sosnowksi's gentle words, and the generous scammer that Sam came across in 'Faith Wallah' is still pages away, waiting to break your heart. No. The fact that you are still here, mired in my tepid prologue, tells me you are a kind Reader. If you were anything like me you would have skipped it long ago. You are no doubt more patient, and wiser, too. Perhaps, then, the mystery of the letter in Will Cox's eponymous story will not elude you, and you will know, straight away, who or what is the unfathomable God of Alexandra McLachlan's 'Sacred Flesh'. Then again, maybe not.

Now, since we appear to have made it together past the first two paragraphs and I still have your attention—for which I am very grateful, I assure you—indulge me a few more words. Just a few, I promise. Allow me to tell you how *Verge*, in its tenth edition, came by the subtitle of 'Everything and Nothing'. It's a funny story.

Originally, we, the editors, did not want *Verge* to have a subtitle. This was discussed on our very first meeting. Our rationale? We did not wish to limit our contributors to a specific topic. Rather, we wanted to showcase talent without restraint. And we wanted to be different too, break with the norm of the last few editions. A few emails ensued, and we realised that a subtitle was perhaps not as limiting as we first thought, and we also had the opportunity of continuing a rather quaint tradition. So, like that famous fiddler inspired by Sholem Aleichem's works who somehow manages to jump from one gable to the next—amid sticky tunes, may I add—without breaking his proverbial neck, we had stumbled upon a challenge. How to be daring and new as we shake hands with the past? How can one be traditional without ceasing to innovate?

The subtitle for this edition comes from a short story by Jorge Luis Borges by the same name. At the end of Borges' 'Everything and Nothing', the story's main character, none other than Shakespeare, lord of all words, stands before God and begs, 'I, who have been so many men in vain, want to be one and myself.' God replies to him from a whirlwind: 'I, like you, am no one; I dreamt the world as you dreamed your works, my Shakespeare, and among the shapes of my dream were you, who, like me, are many people, and no one.'

So, a title need not be a limit; a definition can reverse its function without need for obfuscation (although you wouldn't think that from reading that last sentence!). In art, as in life, if we must girdle ourselves, may that belt be big enough to encompass nothing less than infinity and eternity, the scary confines of the human imagination.

That was our aim, and the result is this book, which, if infinitely more modest, is by no means disappointing. This issue of *Verge* has a mixture of short fiction and poetry, both Australian and international. Some of our contributors are established authors: Coral Bracho, for example is a Mexican poet and translator, a prominent figure of the contemporary neo-baroque. Her three poems 'Deep and Curved Cuts', 'The Vast, Lit, Juniper Tree', and 'It Changes Shape in Ephemeral Moments', are being translated into English for the first time here. There is 'Small Town' by John Tranter, who needs no introduction: his career, spanning over four decades and twenty books has distinguished him in the Australian literary scene. We also have new voices: Emily Riches' and Leah McIntosh's stories 'Unfruitful' and 'The Wading Pool', respectively, won this year's Monash Prize for Creative Writing at the Emerging Writers' Festival. 'Chorus', by talented Australian poet, Anders Villani, twice winner of the John Marsden Prize for Young Australian Writers explores mob mentality. And Internet poets Heiko Julien, Mira Gonzalez, Holly Childs, Emilia Batchelor, Emmie Rae, make our eclectic mix slightly more eclectic. Which is good.

On a final note, I would like to warmly thank my fellow editors, Rebecca Jones and Oscar Schwartz, who are the true architects of this book. Their drive, dedication and support made *Verge* possible this year.

parlous

Stu Hatton

At the far end of an arc, kneeling
by the torch lillies, you possibly
recognise most of your anger as self-

directed. You were the one driving,
were you not? Low on testosterone
and fresh out of nerve hospital,

it's likely to be a long winter, though
you think twice about thinking it.
Soon mushrooms will be sprouting

from dead men's knees—and when did
you last fertilise? The garden gnomes
appear to be posed in some kind of

bacchanalian gangbang, though
it could be your line of sight that
makes it so. Is the garden a free-

speech zone, at least during
peacetime? Is it peacetime? You've
quit keeping tabs on the news, and

those who know you mostly know
not to drone on about anything
that might have you in a fit—

though 'gerontocracy' has proved
a troublesome safeword. You don't
see it as wimping out, though you

have been crouching in the same
spot, like, forever. All the better
to be white-anted, remain blissful

amidst blessèd unrest. All bodies
fall at the same speed, after all—
except for a few large dominants.

The Wrong Side of Saturday

Killian Donohoe

If this were a movie, there'd be some '70s song playing – one that you know, but not by name. Long strides, hands in pockets, shoulders back. I'm wearing a blazer. Eye contact for the ladies, head nods for the lads. I get served pretty much straight away. Whisky sour. I've never had one but I'm not getting a beer. I'm wearing a fucking blazer. No, no, the good stuff. Nineteen bucks and I didn't even flinch. Keep the change. I walk out the back to the outdoor area and spot my mates straight away. No stop, no fake phone check, no scanning the room like a meerkat. Some get handshakes, some get fist bumps depending on the custom of our friendship, but everyone knows what they're doing, and they're happy to be doing it, because I have arrived. Fade music, commence dialogue etc. etc.

I'm on.

I surprise myself by the quick wit of my responses. My jokes land and my stories captivate.

Footy is awesome. Drugs are awesome. Chicks are awesome.

Dave, better known as D 'n' M Dave, shocks nobody when he is the first to broach the subject, asking me how I've been. Whilst we're on the topic of chicks and all.

Pretty good, I tell them. So much time for PlayStation and porn, I tell them. But I wouldn't mind a bit of the real thing, and there are some good sorts around, I tell them. They graciously accept my gift, my pardon, and so we discuss the good sorts and why she is or why she is not hot, and what we'd do and what she'd do...

One of those good sorts smiles at me as I walk out of the bathroom. Of course she does, I'm on.

Then, half by accident, I'm next to her with one elbow on the bar. She turns to me and I ask her to stop objectifying me because it makes me feel uncomfortable. She takes in the smirk, laughs and we're away.

Vodka, lime and soda is an awful drink...

I was there last year. Did you go to...

Oh my God, I love that movie...

When I talk, she smiles. When I've finished, she laughs. When I say things to prompt distilled disgust, she slaps my arm lightly and looks appropriately disgusted.

My mates are at the front door and one catches my eye over her shoulder, tilts his head toward the street and raises his eyebrow to ask the question. I nod, they leave.

The lights go on and everyone shuffles out the front, where they stand in small groups plotting their next move.

We both want another drink, but neither of us know a good place around here. She has drinks at her house.

* * *

She told me that we could try again in the morning, but she knew as well as I did that we were the wrong side of Saturday night and the things we liked about each other last night wouldn't be there this morning.

Our backs formed a valley between us in the bed and I could hear her blink. Yesterday in a Maccas carpark I bought a bag of confidence from a guy with a made up name in an '84 Alfa. I have no doubt that I would not be in this room without it. But the price you pay is that once you get here, there's nothing you can do but apologise and blame the booze. And in a perverse irony that would be funny if I weren't victim to it, you have to lay there with sleep the only thing more out of the question than an erection.

So I look at the curtain, waiting for the glow of morning to creep in the edges so I can inch out of the bed on the back of a plausible excuse that she won't believe but will gladly accept.

The dark recedes slowly but the rattling of a tram outside announces morning or something like it. With my story somewhat straight (Nan's birthday in the country. Darn!) I slowly pull on my jeans, pick up my shoes and blazer and tip toe to the door. I crane my neck to see if she's awake. As though she's fallen asleep during her evening prayers, her cheek rests on both her hands and her eyes are intently closed. It's a caricature of sleep. I know she's saving herself an awkward conversation, but all the same, what a class act. All things going well, I'll never see her again.

Having spent last week's pay and Youth Allowance on whisky, rack and a blazer that looks like it was thrown in with a mid-sized family sedan, I can't afford a cab home, so I walk the ten minutes to Richmond Station. Cold wind whistles down Punt Road and through the platforms above it. Sunday timetable – 25-minute wait. I count ten dollars in coins in my pocket, which I apparently didn't consider currency last night, so I walk to a nearby café braced against the cold.

'Big night, bro?', asks the smiling Ned Kelly-looking hipster who takes my order.

My disdain is naked and unreasonable. I look at him without answering.

I take my first sip back at the platform to find that he hasn't stirred the sugar in my coffee. I'm convinced it's a personal attack. I teeter between rage and sadness that someone would do this to me or to anyone. I take deep breaths and the tears that threaten subside.

At home I sleep, or close my eyes, for a few hours and wake up empty.

D 'n' M Dave calls for details as sordid as I'm willing to reveal. It was awesome, I tell him. She was a fiend, I tell him. Not sure if I'll see her again though, she was a bit clingy, I tell him.

But I don't tell him that I miss Her and that I'm sick of fucking – not fucking – girls as desperate for validation as myself. I don't tell him that being with that girl was like driving on the wrong side of the road – essentially the same but somehow completely different.

My isolation is amplified but I know it's real. I know it will be there tomorrow and that She will not.

I remember being at the pub soon after we broke up.

'You all good?', a mate had asked.

No, I said, breaking rules unwritten but as ironclad as statute. I told him how I checked Her Facebook three times a day and that I was pretty sure She had a new boyfriend and that I was probably going to run him over with my car and that he looked like an arsehole and that She must be doing it to make me jealous so we could get back together.

'Yeah. It's rough', he replied, almost frightened.

He then finished his beer and went to the bar for another. He brought me back a pint. It was some boutique pale ale, rather than the standard domestic. We do what we can.

Rest Is An Obstructed Fall

Mira Gonzalez

you think that motion is only possible by displacement, and

you know that you are moving away from everything, slowly

one second at a time, forever

each second you forget another second

you are thinking about this tendency you have

to rouse untouched anger in people

on long car rides, you are quiet for hours at a time

you know there is something vaguely threatening

when he throws half his body over you

you are almost in danger

you understand then, the feeling of empty space

between qualitatively indistinguishable atoms

you deserve this, you think

because you are nothing special, not really

you focus on a dense and angular void

in the space between his nose and his mouth

Eight Short Poems

Mira Gonzalez

1

if he doesn't make you feel desperate
then you aren't afraid of losing him

2

the only thing anyone ever says is
'please acknowledge that i'm in pain too'

3

how ashamed do i have to feel
before i start enjoying sex again

4

does it feel crippling
when you think about him

5

he tells you the stars in the sky are shaking
and you are honestly on enough drugs to believe him

6

you don't seem like the type to have violent fantasies
so i will need to have enough of them for both of us

7

here are some things i have recently learned about myself,
i only like warm weather and dairy products make me more depressed
and i'm tired of being told i'm not allowed to feel ownership over someone

8

trust me when i say that every hour will become shorter
until hours don't exist anymore

A Coaster for the Jovial

Peter Dawncy

I've just crashed my car into a tree by a river. Bloody and gasping, I try to heave myself from the wreckage. But my door's been smashed in, and pain blazes in my hip and shoulder.

I hear talking, and see three men unfold from the brush in front of me. They each carry a fishing pole. Wobbling their heads as they laugh and poke one another in the cheeks, they perch on my crumpled roof and cast into the middle of the river. The simultaneous plops of sinkers in the quiet water seem distant.

I strain to let my head flop from my broken window, and I try to reason with the men. But the closest, who is deep in conversation, casually opens a big can of beer and places it on my forehead. I become furious and cry out, and try to shake the beer off. But the can is just so heavy, and my neck is so weak, and even in the brief moments when the man has removed the beer, had a swig and replaced it, I've still been too weak to move.

So, moaning and whispering, there I sit: a coaster for the jovial…

The Foolish Tower

Peter Dawncy

You ask me to unpack my mind for a moment. And because it is said that we should not keep secrets from one another, I comply, tipping most of my mind onto the table—keeping just enough so that we may continue to converse rationally. After running your hands over the fragments you start building a tower, giggling at each piece as you turn it over. With my remaining sense I remind you that I have done a faithful and trusting thing in unpacking my mind for you, and say that I would prefer you not laugh at nor undertake such frivolous and precarious activities with something of such importance. You just shrug and take more from my head, and say that I have not the sense to pass such judgement. I inform you that my remaining sense is still of a judicious nature, and with it I ask you to please, once you've finished, have the heart to return my mind, for I know of your tendency to gaze at your own creations and rue their destruction. But now you demand the rest, and lacking all volition, I comply, and you complete the tower with my deepest secrets at the uppermost levels. Then you depart, and I am left a dribbling idiot, peering at the constructs of my folly.

Black Saturday

Peter Dawncy

Land life could not be sustained in such desiccating heat, so we became aquatic for the day and swam in the dam beside the drive at the front of the farm, swinging water-noodles and scooping up backswimmers, piffing a tennis ball and sitting on the inflated oasis chewing mint jellies and strawberry jubes and sipping fizzy fluids through coloured straws. The trees were wheezing in stifling winds, their dangling bark kicking and cracking, parched leaves squinting, and in the gasping paddocks there were plenty of dust devils demanding our attention. Summer clothes flailed and flashed on saplings near the front gate, wallets and watches and electronics protruded from shoes in the bracken beneath, and spare noodles stood kinked and dog-chewed in the adjacent clump of scrambling coral-fern. The water's surface was speckled with pollen from wattles on the dam's eastern edge and the yellow clung to our skin and hair, got in our eyes, ears, nostrils, between our teeth. An arid and booming Mount Dandenong loomed behind us and the swampy valley below shone with the rising heat.

There wasn't enough room on the dam wall for all the cars, so some had to park down the road. Josh caught a mud-eye from the logs by the bull-paddock bank and put it on Sarah's leg: the nymph looked really dark and spiky and evil against the stark white of Sarah's quad, and she certainly thought so too. We saw how many of us could fit on the duck platform just out from the dead blackwoods on the steep slope, but it was a bit anticlimactic because it turned out everyone could easily fit and we stood there silly and dazed, swaying, glistening like strung-up sardines in the searing sun. Near the bulrushes at the deep end we swung in from the rope that we'd tied to one of the blue gum's highest branches the year before. The steaming dirt scorched the soles of our feet when we clambered out. James flew in upside down a few times and no one else could. Cal brought meat pies, sausage rolls, lamingtons and vanilla slices from the Monbulk bakery for lunch and even remembered the sauce. We ate in the shaded water and watched the flakes of pastry that quivered and spun as they drifted down to the overflow. Then it was back into the sunlight to pummel one another with the noodles and skim the tennis ball at each other's heads and see who could dive the deepest for a handful of mud.

We were giddy from the heat and the gusty flour-dry air: the nine preceding days over thirty, three of those over forty, that freakish tenth one close to fifty with something like four percent humidity and hundred kilometre winds. We were stunned by the brightness and the eucalyptus oil that wrought havoc on our sinuses. We had endured twelve years, over half our lives, in drought. We were sunburnt and waterlogged, wrinkled to the bone, frazzled and well-squiffed—lean country boys and girls whose heads had evaporated. We were little more than jostling titbits of flotsam bobbing between the banks of that trembling freshwater mass. Our sky was empty and we were content.

Soon after lunch we capsised the oasis and gathered in the coolness beneath it where our voices creaked and gurgled. Everyone was relishing the sudden proximity, the clutter of bobbing smiles and slimy limbs, the cosy conversations and the smells of fruity shampoos. I found the sudden loss of context disconcerting though, and more than a little frightening: without the trees, the paddocks and the mountain it seemed that the dark water slapping our chins could be any water, anywhere, of any depth, through which any toothy behemoths cruised, and my heart leapt whenever we drifted to a bank or fallen tree and something suddenly dug into my leg.

There was a flash as someone lifted a corner of the oasis and pulled themselves under. They held a lighter and two thin lengths of white above the water. I watched their kinked thumb crank the notched wheel and the sparks were dazzling. Glowing faces went gaunt with each draw, shadows forming in the hollows, and I imagined my own doing the same when my turn came. Creamy tendrils curled and intertwined on the ripples. My head prickled. I tried to focus on the circling dots of crinkled light, sacred light passed with care, rising and dipping, briefly brighter as air was sucked through. Soon my trepidation over the lack of context dissipated and swimming became easier.

She was on the other side, near the big *Oasis* logo, calmly treading water and talking to friends, looking really lovely in the smoky dimness with her dark hair wet and pushed behind her ears. Lauren Jenkins. I imagined the clenched teeth and slitted eyes of her advance before she pushed her way through the sopping lumps towards me. Her voice was soft and her minty breath stung my skin. She bent her hands around my hips as she raised her chin to send a stream of water between my eyes. I held onto the oasis so that she could sling an arm around my shoulders and neither of us had to kick to stay afloat. She dug her fingernails into my neck, bit down on my tongue and gripped my testicles through my shorts until I tensed and yelped.

Lauren has always been a creature of torment for me: a girl as alluring, pleasant and adept as she is devilish. When we used to ride dirt bikes through the paddocks after school, she looked like such an angel atop the burbling heap, all pink-helmeted and pink-gloved, usually wearing tights, her hair whipped high and shiny and her butt sticking right out. Her older brothers had dirt bikes and she was no stranger to one, hurtling along the clumpy cattle-tracks and bullying the bike's handlebars into tight turns round trees and troughs. But she would often dart in front of me, forcing me to swerve, and if already ahead she would sometimes brake suddenly, throw her bike into a low gear and accelerate hard, trying to kick dirt and cowpats my way, usually succeeding.

After hauling in nets of blackfish and short-finned eels from the dam, she would deal with the fish, cleaning and gutting them, while I danced around the eels, trying to herd the hissing things into hessian sacks, their horrible bodies caked with dirt and grit. Dad would barbeque the fish that evening and the three of us would sit on the veranda in the dying light to eat the brilliant white flesh with lemon, salt and cracked pepper. The eels we'd relocate to Sassafras Creek, unless one happened to make it beyond my swinging feet during the herding, in which case it would firstly be relocated down the back of my shirt by a pair of quick, spirited hands and a heated scuffle between boy and beast would ensue. She knew how much I hated eels. It took ages to scrub off the claggy slime in the shower.

I would follow Lauren anywhere without question. She knew this also, much too well, and used it to her cruel advantage. When we went blackberry picking at the end of summer, for instance, she liked to lead me deep into the palaces of vicious green, talking casually, swivelling her hips, stretching her arms up and back and removing layers as the heat increased. I tried to act just as casual, hide her effect on my body and pretend that something about the blackberries and our random turns didn't trouble me. Then, without notice, she would slip away like the breeze and I'd be left lurching through the flashing leaves and bristling tangles, calling her name, shielding my face, blackbirds and starlings screaming at me as they flapped furiously by. The thorny canes shredded my clothes, crowded my sky and ruled my nightmares.

On hearing the crackle of tyres on gravel we emerged from our muggy refuge. The glare and heat were substantially more severe than they'd been and the water was somehow heavier, pressing tighter round my ribs and trying to drag me down. I kicked harder and curled my shoulders as I tried to gulp more air. The blossom on the wattles struck my eyes like blades. Lauren chose this moment to climb onto my back and dunk my head under the water. I inhaled a mouthful and returned spluttering to the surface. While the others swam to greet the newcomer I paddled back to the oasis and hauled myself aboard to clear my lungs. I lay supine with my head to the side, scrunched my eyes shut and rubbed my raw throat. My mouth tasted of bullets. Soon I was quite dry, my hair caked to my upturned cheek and my back glued to the hot plastic.

I can't remember the last time we had heat like this—the kind of dire heat that envelops you in thick swells, floods into your lungs, clamps your heart and oozes through you. The sort of heat that makes you pant and gag, mumble, ache, and feel like a foreigner in your own backyard. The heat that turns thoughts into bright slippery shards and tries to oust you from consciousness. The sort in which birds and beasts cannot be seen, huddled as they are in the coolest pockets of the bleeding woods. And snakes in hot-blooded heaven shriek jubilantly as they run amuck in the abundance of tender flesh. The kind of wrathful heat in which it seems the world is already in flames.

I could no longer hear the voices of the others, nor their swimming. Had they been overcome? Were they no more than little dispersions of limbs and organs in the water? The breeze strengthened and something that smelt like blood stung my nostrils. A few voices came, but distant and muffled. I opened my eyes and turned my head to peer across the windswept stretch to the dam wall: in the shallows by the drive, shiny pink blobs jittered, melded and disjoined; above them, a grey figure stood gesticulating against the stirring tea trees. One of the blobs threw something green to the grey figure and the figure threw the green thing back. I kneaded my eyes with a thumb and forefinger. Who could the newcomer be? All the usuals had been at the dam for hours. Perhaps it was someone's brother or sister.

The oasis rotated in the wind and the dam wall disappeared. The voices went as well. My eyes re-closed. There was some thought I was on the verge of thinking—something urgent, I felt, but couldn't quite grasp. Something obvious. It seemed so palpable at first, right in the roasting middle of me, as though I was already thinking the thing; yet it quickly fled and in its wake left only a trail of faintly associated impressions. And the harder I reached, the more I strained to trace the impressions to the thought, the further away it slipped, until, finally, even the impressions winked out and there was only the strengthening wind and the scything leaves and the rumbling heat before my mind filled with swirling sparks and it was me slipping, coming undone, tumbling from my head into the water and sinking like marbles into the mushy depths. There was an immense turbulence, a broil of bubbles and shadows, and then all was still, icy and oddly serene. Up through the gloom and fractured light I saw my body: a splayed glob of busted skin strewn on the spinning plastic. Black limbs stretched over it and an armada of scrunched-up bark escorted by a few stray noodles drifted away. And in the surrounding spread of pale green sat the dark dots of pollen.

I spotted large silver and golden perch lurking in the tree debris beneath the dam's embankments: fish released as fingerlings by a man and boy years before and through feasting on the dam's thriving society of yabbies, nymphs and water boatmen became plump and lordly. I discerned the same man and boy crouched years later behind the water-scrub with a rod and net, the boy idly pulling apart tufts of sword grass while the man perused a box of lures, attempting to match one to the season and the afternoon's colour. In the greenery, high up the hill behind them, I saw the brickwork of the wifeless, motherless, siblingless house in which they lived—a solitary speck of orange and red in the midst of coarse farmland. Its windows were covered with cobwebs and its garden appeared sparse.

As the man lifted various hook-laden fish and insect imitations to the light his expression was twisted in crinkled concentration, his brow low, lips drawn up tight and eyelids puckered. It was that classic farmer's face with the rough waves and whorls of flesh, with the dusty whiskers and the busted capillaries, the gnarls and dips and crumpled belts, and eyes like sunrises. But the steeliness, the tenacity, the rolling skin—it wasn't so much a face at all, but more like some wise and resilient creature he'd caught in a swamp, set on his skull and pitted against the pitiless years. And what a wonder that such walnutty hands, so accustomed to hefting and lugging, could show such delicate craft in their tying of a lure to fishing line. Hands that in the sprawling hills and dizzying heat were always there to steady and guide and nourish. In that heaving bucolic world he was weather-watcher and bonfire-builder, fence-fixer and wood-splitter, water-pumper, thistle-killer, tree-planter and cow-healer. He was the helpful fellow down the road, the ever-loyal friend, the warm and tolerant father and the man whose love for the land slowly filled the void left by the early death of a wife. Despite his customary stoicism the loss of my mother took its toll, and even in his later years he was often overwhelmed by a frightening grief and faded for a time—became no more than a hay bale surrounded by hungry cows, a cassinia in the bush beyond the far fence, an algae-filled pond in the middle paddock's windbreak, a cocoon of web caught on an idle tractor beneath a sky of cracked clouds and whirling colours. And on finally finding this strange and sneezing creature in my searching I sat nearby and wept as well, watched dusk sweep in over the jumbled slopes and huddled scrub, stared at the coming stars, listened to the wind in the grass, and the wood ducks, calling.

When the others returned I learned that the grey figure on the drive was not a newcomer seeking admission to the cool water, but my father stopping to say a few words before he departed. He looked worried and tired, they said, and he spoke quickly, but still smiled when they threw the tennis ball to him. He told them he was heading to Denny's horse farm near Narbethong—apparently there were fires up north. He said the sprinklers and hoses at our house were all prepped and that we should switch to ABC Radio in one of the cars. And watch for smoke. It also might be a good idea for some people to head home, he'd said. I lay there peering at the sky. Josh splashed water over me and I told him he could be such a shit sometimes. Someone wondered whether it was time to get out the water volleyball set and everyone agreed that this was a good idea.

We'd been invited to a party in Emerald that night and there wasn't a chance we weren't going. When everyone else had left the dam I went with Lauren back up to the house to eat. Dad still wasn't home and wasn't answering his phone, so I put a note on the bench saying where we'd be. Denny and Dad went way back and were probably just having dinner or looking over the horses. The few fires in Victoria didn't sound too bad from the news reports, and none were close. Every year before summer the Emergency Services seem to have a big hoo-ha about how severe the fire season will be, but I think that's just something they have to do.

We left at about eight, picked up Sean from round the corner, Sophie from Kallista and then went booting up the hill to get Benny from the end of Ridge Road. As we passed a group of dog-walkers Sean pummelled the side of the car and barked at them—he does a pretty convincing dog and Sophie couldn't stop laughing. When he brought his face back in he asked if we could stop at the bottle shop in Emerald and I told him that wouldn't be a problem. A few moments later Lauren opened the sunroof and took off her seatbelt so that she could stand and stick her head out. Of course Sophie had to join her and accidentally kneed me in the shoulder as she clambered into the front. The wind thumped in my ears.

Near John's Lookout at the top of the hill we saw lots of people lining the fence beside the bitumen. They were all gazing north, some of the kids wearing pyjamas. It reminded me of New Year's Eve when crowds gathered up there to watch the pyrotechnic displays around the Yarra Valley and south towards the bay. When we reached the clearing we looked out and saw dense clouds glowing a deep red beyond the Great Dividing Range, as though infernal monsters had come on a comet and were waging battle just over the lip of the distant hills. After passing the people I had to pull over. Sean asked what the hell was going on and said something about Damo and Briggsy already being there. We climbed from the car and joined the end of the line on the fence. The temperature had cooled substantially—it actually felt a bit cold by this time. The voices around me were soft and I couldn't understand them. The faces were just pale blotches. Were they Lauren's arms? The valley ahead was dark and east and west were dark and it was just that swirling red.

Incident

Anne Elevy

Upright and vivid, your green curve of plumed flesh is shaped
over bone. Your head tilts. Approaching, I wonder if flight is
possible, if, breathing thing, you are already maimed. I slow,
adjust my course, reckon to avoid the sound of breast

burst, the shock of the heart under a wheel. Inevitably, the car
proceeds. The traffic forbids a merciful turn. I stop at Woolies,
drive through the carpark and around the long block, pull up
in Armstrongs Road, walk back beside the highway. On the
bitumen

there's almost no trace of green in the smear. In each bare pause
between cars, I click, I click. Five times on the mobile phone. On
review, the first picture centres on a mark beneath a lacework of
shadow. A coastal banksia supplies your shroud. For candles, the
lowering sun's long streamers of light spill through the foliage
onto the spot, like an old film's heaven. The camera

shows more than I saw: the business that brought us to the
highway; your altered flesh.

Small Town

John Tranter

You are mad to mourn alone. – Anne Carson

In this town, death creeps day by day
and claims a victim each day.
This is the Small Town of the Blank Wall
where a monster came and went
and where another walked up and down the road.

This is the Small Town of the Useless Police,
who do nothing, protect us from nothing.
It's too hard, they complain, and empty spaces
grow between their solid words of complaint,
their grievous anguish.

Stand up straight. Learn how to be a real man.
This is the Small Town of the Empty Windows
that watch us from a distance. The old man
walks before the cruel child, who quickly grows into
his own father, and shoots from hiding.

But here is not here, it is nowhere. It is where
you know you must be very quiet:
outside the town a frightened rabbit
hops across the highway.
There is nothing on or in the old wood stove.

Killing people out of town is not a sin,
not if a properly elected government asked
or ordered you to do it. As for us, it's different for us.
As for you, weak you, you might as well go
to where the cold moon shines on the forests.

On the moonlit pampas, they take out their knives
and stare at me. A century or more I have waited
for this man with the knife, who listens carefully
to the wind, with his weapon, who takes aim
and impales the moonlight itself.

When I was twenty-five I had learned to say no
to the ugly man with his huge questions and his sack of
stuff, and his tales of blackness waiting just outside
town, outside the world. I wonder
if I really can say no,

no to the deep water running out, under the moon,
its blade of light flickering on the water,
a threat. Like this ugly man who brings
his dark questions and doesn't tell it
like it is.

They ordered me to stop, so I did – where
the river runs deep. Now, I say nothing, when
I have a secret to keep, two words,
like the words 'his car', that I saw
in back of the dark woods.

Sorry; my mistake. Wow, what a lovely day!
Your breakfast is ready: coffee, bacon and
two poached eggs. The cowboys stored
their dreams and hopes where
all the useless hopes were,

otherwise they might become lost in the current
where the little twig wobbles back and forth,
pointing at me, then at you. Yes, it's a lovely day.
I'll tell you what: you pause,
and I'll nip into town.

See the gopher run back into his hole?
The running motion proves he's alive.
Yes, like you, he has a mother
who thinks of him every single day.
To her, he's like a nest-egg of solid gold.

World of Sentient Beings

John Wilkinson

In rising their spread adjusts.
        Might you have felt angelic,
flesh creature, scrounging round the scrap
        accoutrements, the earth-
bound vehicles whose entry failed –
                        but fain
        to rise angelically
unknown to itself goes on to importune,
                        revealing
only spread without limit,
        only universal fledge. Revolving
far beyond the tally,
keep your eye fixed – revoking,
        watch the flea launch, reenter,
unscrutinised the irritating earth
        opalises, pearlises,
        swathes itself in glorious negligence.

Cease fretting at why being here nor there:
        the pimpiest, the leather-
girt outrider, chevron of slew red,
        ellipse of skeins
strung with ironical greetings cards'
        all-too-common poke,
        these cut through fluffed-out

curtained, moiré or glaucous light,
caramelise the ripple, mess the overlap,
        candying a would-be
nub, the nut-hard carapace that springs off
        flea-exact
or exactly brinks. Jump to that.
A swan's wing might break your arm.
A flock of angels might smash the cities
into their component mouth-dams or casts
or thimbles or braces –
        shards that forget their forms
through shivering ecstatically.

Various are the longed-for breaks
and swarming with their intellectual
residents, leaning to insinuate
the same animal smarts, clumping to scrape
incautious hands with mineral
bait-&-switch,
        the fury of the fossils
visible only through the galvanism
rising between cheeks like working mouths,
set in foreheads like loggias open to
collapsed plumes,
acceding through the bone with feelers
scratching at the tympanum,
feathers pelt down as transfixing arrows.
        Faces angle up,
        clouds crawl over them
and they are made general, made boilerplate.

Angels form
into clouds, clouds into shelves. The fog-
horn booms and shakes to the surface

naked, ravenous and violent
        scrunched hard babies.

Gardening With My Business Associate

Nick Modrzewski

I will save you a lot of guessing and just come out with it now: I am in love with my business associate. He is thirty-nine years old and has French ancestry. I love him a little less than I love myself, but only a little. He wears perfectly fitting suits and handmade cufflinks. If I could be alone with my business associate, I would tie him up and talk softly to him, or maybe I would kiss his mouth. These are both things I read about in a book called *Floral Forager*, but they are not really things I want to do myself. Personally, I would like to just talk to him about gardening, because gardening is something I am really interested in and if we can get the sex stuff out of the way and just talk gardening then that'd be great, thanks.

I wait for my business associate in The Marble Cathedral. To find me, my business associate will pass through a giant arch and then walk straight down a hallway lined with plastic plants. The Marble Cathedral is also referred to as The Plastic Shadow Paradise or The Land of Marble Pillars, but its most common name is The Marble Cathedral. Inside, there are many brands and commercial outlets such as *Loran's*, *Air-Plus*, *Declico* and a strip of shops selling coffins at cost price. On both the East and West walls, up high amongst the giant marble blocks, are one hundred and twenty-two square windows. At dawn and dusk each day, a congregation of robed worshipers gather to witness the light pour in.

I see my business associate rushing down the hallway towards me and he looks very handsome, but his hair is ruffled and his shirt is un-tucked. He drops onto the marble bench next to me, his papers spilling from his briefcase.

'That's it,' he says, 'no more of anything for me. No more of anything for poor Randolph. Time to sleep.'

He curls into a ball and begins to sob. It's lucky we're important businessmen or we'd likely be arrested.

'Stop it, Randolph,' I say.

Some important businesswomen at a nearby shop are looking at us. I take out my clipboard and make it look like I'm writing notes. I'm a very busy man doing some busy things.

'I'm over,' he says, 'I'm finished.'

'It's really fantastic you could make it, Randolph,' I say, placing my hand on his shoulder, 'you're a very important businessman and an asset to the company. Let's have a drink to celebrate your intelligence and diligence.'

I gesture to a waiter. There are many waiters roaming The Marble Cathedral, each one representing his own individual beverage company. Competition for clients is fierce and the waiters are tired. They are tired of carrying drinks and they are tired because they are not allowed to sleep. They work for up to two days at a time. It is expected that they faultlessly obey important businessmen, like us, who often request that they dance or do tricks. Today, I simply make the waiter stand on one leg while he receives our orders.

'According to my schedule,' I say, 'we should start by discussing current market structures and the potential elevation of the company within these structures.'

'Current market structures!' says Randolph, 'Of course! My wife says to me: you know Janus? I say: no I don't know Janus, so she says: he's a Roman God, the god of Beginnings and Transitions. He has two faces, they call him the Two Faced Man, the Ugly Split Cell Twin, The Siamese Friend. He visits me in my room at night and makes love to me against my will. But I like it, I like it more than you, Randolph, because he's a passionate lover and kisses me like he wants to crawl through my mouth and dance inside me forever.'

'A daring woman,' I say, 'a woman who knows what she wants.'

'So I say to her: Yemini, you get out of my house, you leave this house right now. So she takes her suitcase and she goes! She's off, she's out of there.'

'Where?'

'She walks out the door – my fox is gone. My parrot is dead. I cannot live like this. Take me with you,' he's hanging off my shirt, 'take me somewhere to die.'

'We must remember,' I say, 'at times like this, to remain calm and in control and not be driven entirely by passion. Let us consider the agenda, for instance, which recommends that by 5:15pm we should have erected a structure for approaching private donors with the aim of establishing philanthropic gifts.'

He's crying out his nose, all over my shirt.

'Where is Yemini now?'

'I don't know. I don't know that. I don't have the money or the experience to know that. And this 'Janus' gave her hundreds of different disguises.'

'Well,' I say, 'if you're feeling upset, why don't we begin by skipping point one, Market Structures and go straight to Regulation of Pricing Policies?'

A small congregation has gathered in the centre of The Marble Cathedral and as the light of the setting sun creeps through the windows, a chorus of sobs and prayers begins.

* * *

My passion for Randolph comes in strong bursts, which usually happen when I'm alone in my bedroom, or walking the streets at night. His image comes to me, naked and dancing, sending me into a trance. I speak aloud and write notes that come from a place I've never been before:

> 'Spinning belly dancer, free Animal Man, wheeling hips and legs that wrap around me. Climb my back and press together, you stalking cat of the night-time.'

I am not, by the way, a homosexual. The voice that uses these words isn't mine. If I could pin it down I'd probably just strangle it and return to reading about gardens.

After discussing some items on the Agenda, including point 3.b. Evaluation of Internal Management, Randolph moans some more about his wife. He is obsessed, it seems, with this 'Janus' figure, and reads out an Encyclopaedia entry about how 'the two faces of Janus indicate that he looks both to the past and the future. He is the God of gates, transitions, and time.'

I say that we should try to find his wife - maybe we can track down this Janus and demand his wife back? We could, I suggest, seek her out in one of the many hundreds of gardens surrounding The Marble Cathedral. This suggestion is, I must admit, a little self-interested. Being alone with Randolph in the gardens would be an excellent opportunity to impress him with my garden knowledge.

'There's no point,' he says, 'she's gone gone gone. Forever. Hundreds of gardens. A woman wearing a hundred disguises in a hundred gardens. Janus. There's no point.'

I stand and take his hand.

'Randolph, I know these gardens better than anyone. Trust me.'

* * *

We arrive at the Threshold to The New French Gardens, where a single guard sleeps at his post. Through the giant gates we see a fountain, pillars, and a long stretch of carefully managed trees. The ground is, of course, covered in concrete. The New French Gardens reject the wildness of typical English Gardens, with their winding paths and unruly shrubbery. During the creation of The New French Gardens, there was much debate on what the landscape should look like and where inspiration should be drawn. All the big names had something to say, and a surge of gardening books hit the market. *Sketches and Hints on Landscape Gardening* by Humphrey Repton caused a stir, as did Gerard Cutler's *Le jardin français*? and Sheildstone's infamous *Some Unconnected Musings On Gardening*. On one side, there was the argument that the formal French garden was an example of 'princely mockery.' Georges Salliard hit back that:

> '...it is not the 'liberty' of savages we should emulate in our gardens. Instead, we should look to the example provided by the French, who, in their delicate arrangements, display man's ability to order and isolate the more beautiful parts of nature.'

Hills were levelled and they uprooted the provocative Kent tree, with its spindly arms that reached out like a sex pest. They dug roughly nine meters into the ground and filled the area with concrete. Marble statues of French citizens were erected and they built long galleries lined with trees, hedge mazes and small, unassuming ponds.

'Follow me,' I whisper, careful not to wake the guard who would no doubt interrogate us. It would arouse suspicion, surely, two important businessmen gallivanting around The New French Gardens with no specific business to attend to other than the retrieval of a wife.

'Where do we go now?' asks my business associate.

The gardens span for hundreds of miles in every direction. If we were to walk in one direction for long enough – a few days, probably – we would eventually reach a giant wall. We would be unable to climb over this wall due to its immense height and the copious amounts of barbed wire. However, we could amuse ourselves by peering through one of the many windows to look upon The Outer Gardens, which stretch for a further hundred or so miles in every direction.

'This way,' I guess, and point towards a fountain. The weather is always pleasant here. It never rains and the sun is friendly. It is always 't-shirt weather,' to quote Hemington's *Conspiracies Surrounding Tropical Gardening*, where he argues that the climate of The New French Gardens is monitored and adjusted by a certain ruling entity. Hemington is careful not to use the word 'God,' but his beliefs are clear even to the most inattentive reader.

My strange lover trudges behind me, his eyes downcast and his briefcase swinging by his side. He looks like a tired salesman.

'You should cheer up,' I say, 'it will make for better luck. The Gardens may even look favourably upon us.'

'Superstitions,' he says, 'I don't have time for superstitions.'

'Not superstitions,' I say, 'I've read that the gardens are extremely responsive to the moods of visitors.'

'Lies,' he says.

Probably lies, I think, but I want to see my lover happy. He stops walking.

'Why are we walking in this direction?' he says.

'Why not?'

'I thought you knew where you were going. We're meant to be following the trail of that cretin, Janus. Where's my wife?'

'You have to understand,' I say, 'that the Gardens do not respond well to logic. Whether we go this direction or that direction – it doesn't matter. If we find your wife it will be due to luck and fortune and faith and coincidence and it will have nothing to do with a plan. Read Nelson, *The Anti-Logic of The New French Gardens*, or alternatively try *Disposable Directions – The Modern Garden*. Or, if you don't have access to these books or the time to read them, just trust me. And give me a smile.'

* * *

Both of us wear big false smiles and walk hand in hand. My business associate swings his briefcase like a child.

We pass a nondescript pond – a lazy pond – a pond that insults no one and which, really, contributes nothing to conversation. If you were to zoom in on this pond from, say, a satellite, you would be disappointed. There are thousands of other ponds in The New French Gardens that look very similar. Actually, it's almost impossible to describe this pond due to its complete lack of distinctiveness. The best word to describe it is 'grey.' It's neither black nor white; strong nor weak. It's hardly worth noting, and there is little to say about it other than that we passed it, and so it forms a checkpoint for our journey. But having said that, it could be argued that any of the ponds, trees, walls, statues or fountains found within The New Gardens could serve as checkpoints.

'Nice pond,' says Randolph, pointing to it.

Finally we emerge from the labyrinth of fountains and ponds and reach a massive grey expanse, like a carpet of storm clouds seen from an aeroplane.

'Must we cross it?' he asks.

'We must cross it.'

'We'll go mad.'

'Hold onto your thoughts and we should be fine.'

'Hold onto your thoughts?'

'Think safely. We'll reassure each other – we'll talk about business and things that make us feel safe.'

'Like spreadsheets.'

'Or meetings.'

'What about calculating billable hours?'

'That too.'

Randolph takes a deep breath.

We enter the concrete desert with the pleasant sky smiling on us. Immediately I feel lightheaded. My body starts to swim and words swell inside me.

'It is a joy to order a large body of data,' I say, trying to compose myself.

'Indeed,' says Randolph, 'to file printed text into different categories and arrange them according to their date is a pastime I enjoy.'

He knows I've been affected and he's rattling off statistics about company growth to help me hold onto my thoughts but I can barely stand straight and all of a sudden I hear the voice returning.

'I love you,' I shout, grabbing his shoulders, my words terrifyingly pure and true and uncontrollable, 'you are a dangerous lover with irresistible cheeks.'

'Mathematics,' shouts Randolph, 'seven times three equals fifty one!'

'If you want to make a mailing list of different clients,' I cry, 'you create a column in Excel by dragging the cursor over a vertical line off your shoulders, they make me salivate in winter.'

'What?'

'I want to watch you shower.'

The words are shooting off in different directions like madmen playing soccer, kicking the ball at each other.

Suddenly Randolph grabs me by the hips and I see he's lost his mind too, his pupils dilated like he's staring into the eyes of God and he's sweating. He delicately touches my nose, his eyes horrified by his hands.

'Beautiful…man,' he says, the words exiting his mouth uncomfortably like regurgitation.

'Wonderful lover,'

'Springtime dancer.'

'Kisses,' and our mouths lock, sealed together with sweat. Our eyes try not to stare at each other.

The type of love I'd like to practice is a much more conversational love where we discuss the influence of Palladian architecture in English gardens. But in this moment, embracing my business associate's mouth, I cannot help but feel a sense of warmth, like this is absolutely the right thing to do. The gardens spin around us and something reminds me of a dream. We are going deeper into a reality I don't understand or trust. I accept this madness. I let my body move to its own course and I close my eyes. I surrender entirely to this single sweaty moment and I feel his body loosening too. We sway in a slow dance.

I gently pull my mouth away.

'Anyway,' he says, 'let's find that wife of mine.'

'Of course,' I say, 'wives are an important thing.'

'They are important for any man.'

'All the more important for important business men, like us.'

'Exactly. Like us.'

* * *

The next few hours we walk in silence. Randolph stays a good fifty or so meters in front of me, turning his head every so often. My mind feels like it's been wiped clean or lifted from my skull so that everything I observe is fresh. This suited figure walking ahead of me swinging his briefcase is no longer nameable. He has surpassed flesh and exists only in theory, in a place just beyond words like a name on the tip of a tongue. I consider writing a book about him:

Hints and Sketches on Gardening Inside My Business Associate

My Business Associate – Jardin?

Ahead of me, my business associate halts. He turns around. He walks towards me, stopping when he is directly in front of my face.

'When we find Yemini I'd very much like it if you go away,' he says.

'Away?'

'Away. Yes.'

'Where would you like me to go?'

'Oh, I don't know. Over there, for instance.'

He points into the grey distance.

'How will you find your way out of the Gardens?

'We'll figure it out.'

His face is red, he is sweating even though the day is pleasant and I feel oddly calm, receiving this information.

'Are you upset about what happened earlier?'

'No.'

'You're upset.'

'I'm not upset.'

'Your face is red.'

'No it's not.'

'I love you.'

The gardens are inside him and they are inside me too. I feel the logic dribbling away, the madness of the moment in my eyes. My hands are infected with Garden. I have the confidence of a man who knows what he wants. I want to grapple his neck like a delicate wrestling move.

'You love me,' I say, 'you've always been in love with me.'

My business associate is backing away from me now. I kiss him and he pushes me.

'My wife!' he cries.

'You don't have a wife.'

'What?'

'You made it up so we could be alone here, together.'

'Spreadsheets. Mathematics!'

'It's useless,' I say, 'you are my business associate and I am yours. I am in love with you and I will tie you up and whisper things to you about gardens.'

He grabs my hair and kisses me.

I imagine this is how it feels not to think at all.

* * *

Eventually, we give up the search for Yemini and, due to a series of fortunate coincidences, escape from The New French Gardens.

My business associate maintains that his wife does exist and that he did not make her up in order to be alone with me. He says he loves his wife very much, and he is still distraught about her running off with Janus, the two-faced Roman God of Transitions and Gates. However, he tells me that the moments he and I shared on the great grey plane were not simply instances of irrationality. There is a part of him that loves me in an inexplicable way, the way that exists between two business associates and which manifests itself, sometimes, in kissing.

At first I feel cheated, and I tell him he can't just go around loving people willy-nilly. I imagine him having sex with his wife while I wait at the end of the bed with my clipboard, taking business notes.

I say: 'It's me or her, Randolph.'

And he says: 'my love for Yemini doesn't effect the way I love you.'

Seeing as I don't really want to have sex with him anyway, I concede that perhaps this split love is possible. Perhaps I need to close my eyes to the parts of our relationship that do not concern me, that are none of my business, really.

We agree, over lunch at our next Executive meeting, that our business is in a period of transition.

Deep and Curved Cuts

Coral Bracho

Translated by Gabriel Garcia Ochoa

Shadows cast from the pine's thin branches
coil
around its trunk
and take root in it.
Deep and sinuous cuts
that ought to separate it with one blow,
ought to make it fall,
but only at this hour,
under this precise angle of the rays of the sun
and only if it were to lose, suddenly, and during that hour,
its firm confidence.

The vast, lit, juniper tree

Coral Bracho

Translated by Gabriel Garcia Ochoa

The tree that opens to the sky and wind
with tangled branches,
dense, shapely branches
that flow
and are drenched in shadows,
that burn from the earth,
and rise, that make their tall fire
take root in the earth, their tall flames;
this soft tree that opens like an offering
and radiates; that guards
between its bark,
and the gilded tale
of its resin
the sun;
this tree that names, that unfolds its impulse
like a prophecy, a breath
that embodies
and its inscrutable strength;
this igneous tree, vast,
beloved,
and brief.

It changes shape in ephemeral moments

Coral Bracho

Translated by Gabriel Garcia Ochoa

A fictitious bird, a bait,
shaped with the arboreal
and minute branches of the cypress,
supported by two thin branches
in the midst of its dense foliage;
a calm space, with the outline of a house,
whose illusory wall touches
this, house that is almost illusory
too, the threshold
where I am.
That majestic, albeit brief bait,
that carries on its head a tiara
and draws a peaceful outline
in and outside of itself,
in ephemeral moments it changes shape,
but comes back afterwards–untouched–
to its true majesty.
That bait, then–at times a mouse–
opens and closes its beak incessantly
to alert, to say everything,
to express the nothingness that is everything,
and how little it values hierarchies.
above all, it says, now–clearly upset–

those that separate,
what is supposedly unreal
from what, even more supposedly so,
isn't.
Now that it has finished talking
it changes its shape, slightly,
and is more of a worried and incisive mouse
or a little horse–or a seahorse–
than the sovereign bird of thunderous gaze
which is supported, yet again, at the very centre,
the levitating centre,
of a house.

The City of Jasmine

Marika Sosnowski

Today is my birthday. I am an old man. I have been in this city a long time and I am not going to leave despite all that has happened. I will die here, probably quite soon, and our long connection with this ancient city will be swept away. I want to tell you our story before it is too late.

I am Yehud ash-Sham.

Starting at the beginning is difficult. Like many families and communities, history inevitably becomes an embellished truth. It's because we never marked the beginning with anything, so now it's difficult to know how it all really began. The collective diary entry of when Jews arrived in Damascus has been lost and mythologised in the consciousness of the Jewish people and of my family.

I have been told that the origins of my family lie in the Jewish dispersal and exile from Jerusalem following the destruction of the first temple by Nebuchadnezzar over 2500 years ago. My forebears fled Jerusalem and settled in what was then the fledgling city of Damascus. On their way so many soldiers were patrolling the roads that the family was forced to take refuge in a haystack for fear of being found and killed as a result of their religion. The family of five hid there for several days until they thought it safe to continue. It was a hard time. Because they kept kosher all they could eat was a small amount of dried bread and nuts they had stashed in their pockets when they fled their home leaving everything else behind. For three days they lived like this, huddled there in the middle of the haystack, until finally they emerged, hungry, tired and sore and set off to walk the rest of the way along the Northern Road to Damascus. With the military patrols, the winter weather and the bandits, how they managed to arrive at all remains a mystery.

Their original plan was to keep on to Babylon because of the vibrant Jewish community already there, but once they arrived in Damascus, purely by chance, they met up with some extended family and neighbours from Jerusalem and felt inclined to stay.

At that time, business was picking up in Damascus. From humble beginnings, when my family arrived, the city was assuming the mantle it has carried more or less ever since. Each day dozens of caravans led by exotic Chinese, Indians and Persians carrying spices, silks and steel passed through the old Roman city gates in search of food, shelter and commerce. Once inside the old city they went on to the *khans* where their wares were sold in bulk to the highest bidder. From there the products were sold on to various stallholders in the *souks* around town. For enterprising Jews, it was not at all a bad place to lay down some roots.

Of course, no one can say with any certainty that this is how my family's connection with Damascus began. Archeologists and historians tell us there is evidence of the presence of Jews in the old city at this time and, it of course, flatters my family's sense of itself not to question this narrative. Also, the Syrian government is not about to open up any ancient documents it is holding in its archives to prove otherwise so my family currently holds the balance of power in this regard. But times are changing.

And they went to Damascus and lived there and made him king in Damascus.
First Book of Kings 11:24

My own connection with Damascus began in 1917. I was born here in the last year of what is now known as the Ottoman Empire. When I was born, the rule of the Ottoman's from Istanbul and their local *Pasha* was all anyone alive knew. Jews were not accepted per se but there was a certain respect for our religion and social practices if we just made sure to pay our taxes on time. That said, even though my religion is Jewish, I am certainly an Arab. My first language is Arabic, my second Hebrew.

We have a house in the Al-Amin neighbourhood, just down the road from the Jobar Synagogue. Al-Amin is the Jewish Quarter and the synagogue was our second home. As a child I used to run to the large outer wooden doors and rush in, to find men, only men, animatedly discussing tracts of the Torah or the Mishnah, the state of politics or the price of bread. I sat on the floor with the other children underneath ancient leadlight ceilings in the library and read. I love it there. Being simultaneously part of the ancient, old, dead past and also the vibrant, noisy, alive now.

Sometimes my best friend Ahmad Ghaneim would race in, grab me and tell me that the sweet maker Fouad Mousa had just made a new batch of *ghazi el banat*. I'd leave my book and race outside to join him in the crisp air of winter Damascus. We'd run through the streets in order to try to secure a place towards the front of the line so we could get the fairy floss while it was still warm. *Shami* kids had been doing exactly the same thing for centuries, I am sure.

After we'd gotten our floss we'd go down to the courtyard in front of the Umayyad Mosque and eat it while we watched people pass by. I can still feel the way the thick pink strands of sugar tickled the sides of my nose and stuck to my mouth as I ate them. Most passers-by would go into the mosque to pray. Others would turn right down Straight Street in order to sit at the Rashid Club, one of the most popular in town, play backgammon and smoke the *sheeshah*. Sometimes when we'd walk home that way, I'd see my father sitting there, playing and chatting.

On 31 March 2013 the Jobar Synagogue was burned and looted.

As I grew, it became time for me to attend the Maimonides school in Beit Lisbona just round the corner from the Jobar Synagogue. There were about 1000 boys in my school and about 1000 girls in the girls' school at Beit Farhi. Many were Jews. We learned Arabic at school and also had classes in English and French. There were Hebrew lessons for the Jewish children like me, and we also learnt Hebrew at the synagogue. I remember my mother complaining sometimes about the secular subjects we learnt, like music, craft and mathematics. My father would chuckle and tell her that our family had to join the wider world at some point. During the occupation, he had learnt French himself from officers stationed in Damascus as well as from books. He often came to pick me up from school in order to chat with my teacher who was from Paris. I think he enjoyed the practice, and, in hindsight, perhaps he liked to show off his worldliness to the other parents just a bit.

After school, synagogue and a little play, I'd arrive home for dinner. This would often mean a meal cooked by my mother and aunt in the *tandoor*. Most food had to be cooked at home if you kept kosher as we did. The *tandoor* was used for grilling and roasting fresh chicken as well as for stews. My mother would buy the chicken from the market during the day and have it killed, plucked and filleted while she waited. As I walked home from school I could smell the roasting chicken, flavoured with garlic and mint, drifting down the street, drawing me home.

On Friday night, like Jews everywhere, we ate chicken soup and rice and on Shabbat we ate dishes that had been prepared before the sabbath came in, like meat dumplings in an okra stew and perhaps lamb. If we were really lucky there'd be a delectable treat appropriately named *manna.* It was made from tamarisk and almond cream and to me, it did seem like it came directly from heaven.

Often on Shabbat and other high holy days we'd leave the city and go to the Ghouta with food, arak and musical instruments to eat, drink and sing. Sometimes my friend Ahmad Ghaneim and his family would come along even though they weren't Jewish. Ahmad and I would run around playing hide and seek between the plum trees in the orchards. We'd climb the trees to pick the fruit and often go home with a stomachache. In that season, the Ghouta was always lush and green and I felt free being able to roam without a care in the world.

We'd arrive home in the evening, and if it was warm enough, we would sleep on the roof, where it was cooler. No rain, thousands of stars, the scent of jasmine.

On 21 August 2013 a chemical weapons attack occurred in the Ghouta.

My parents were first cousins once removed and so were my father's parents. It was common in those days. People were conscious of class strata and afraid of the unfamiliar and so tended to marry those they knew well.

I was criticised by many for the way I married. I met my wife while on a business trip to Aleppo. We went together for four years as friends and got married in 1942. At the engagement party we served sugared almonds and Turkish delight. Relations from Aleppo attended who had the famous *Halabi* talent for singing. They sang ancient Aleppine hymns, many in Arabic. There was a certain lightness to them when they were sung as a *mitzvah,* as they were for us. It was an elegant way of breaking down the friendly rivalry that was often present between *Halabis* and *Shamis.* They sang long into the night and my wife and I felt very blessed to have them with us. All those that attended spoke of the singers for many days afterwards.

For the wedding, as custom had it, we arranged a small table at the entrance to the synagogue, upon which sat a white satin bag embroidered with gold. This is where the guests put their gifts, mostly coin. After the wedding my bride donned thick gold anklets and had gold tassels plaited in her hair. It was the most amazing moment of my life - seeing her there, resplendent in white and gold. She looked just like an angel.

Since July 2012 Aleppo has been effectively divided by fighting - one half is controlled by regime forces and the other by rebels.

It seemed world events had finally caught up with us as my father had wished when the state of Israel was founded in 1948. After the 1948 war that accompanied Israel's birth the Syrian government passed laws effectively seizing Jewish property. Unsurprisingly, such measures made many nervous and a great number of people emigrated immediately to the fledgling state of Israel leaving behind their money, property and business assets. Many of their homes were taken over by Palestinian refugees. The rest were appropriated by the state.

I remember the police searching our house. If they found anything to do with Zionism or Israel they would arrest you. I remember my mother having beautiful bedspreads she had made herself that the *shabiha* ripped apart before our eyes. We'd already burnt any documents or books that contained Modern Hebrew and other, rarer books, that belonged to an eminent Rabbi relation of my mother. I remember my mother crying.

After the 1967 war everyone in the Jewish community was watched by the *shabiha* at home, work and shule. Our passports were withdrawn, making us virtual prisoners in our own country. In the years that followed hundreds of community members were imprisoned by the regime. Easily fifty or sixty were taken from their homes and killed. I had just taken over as President of the community and I could only save three men. I wrote to the President many times but the reply was always the same – they didn't know what had happened to the missing men.

In these years, for the main festivals of *Rosh Hashanah*, *Yom Kippur* and *Pesach*, I would try to organise a rabbi to visit from Turkey. If the government did not issue his visa, someone in the community would conduct the services. Since 2000 we have not had much need of a rabbi. There have been no *bar mitzvahs* or weddings as there are no Jews left to marry.

In May 2012 it was reported that only 22 Jews still lived in Syria.

I will end soon and so will the Jewish presence in Damascus. Unfortunately, my birthday has not stopped the current troubles reaching right to my door. I thank G-d that my parents are long dead and that my wife passed from cancer the year the protests began. My friend Ahmad Ghaneim has left for Lebanon with his family. No one wants to see this city, their beloved city for generations, torn apart, culture by culture, building by building, limb by limb.

There are few now left in the community, and those that have stayed fear for their lives. I don't fear. It is nearly over anyway and I have faith that the Jewish ability to survive and start again comes from generations of experience.

Beautiful Cakes

Michael Farrell

Changing his name
Was the one most decisive
Thing in making him happier on a day-
To-day basis. It also boosted his career. Who
Wouldn't want to go to a reception or gala or
Party graced with the presence of Beautiful
 Cakes?
 In Rome he
Went by the Italian Belle Torte
But loved nevertheless to add the
Translation, even though it was the original name, of
This version of himself anyway. However it could be said
Belle Torte was subtly – saccharinely – different to
Beautiful Cakes. Later
That night in the farmyard: or
Was it a sewer? he was giving a
Tour of gravestones, adding his usual flourish, when he
Passed a hairdressers. A man inside had the sweetest scissor
Movement and Beautiful Cakes
Had an image
Of him cutting through pizza and
Then his own heart in the
Form of a castle. Queens and princes came out
Like sleepy blackbirds, some with heads and arms missing. 'Where
Has our wisdom gone?' they sang yawningly

Life

Michael Farrell

The serial number on the machine is now
Part of it. Coffee needn't be
The next image, it could be a random
Piece of rust or dirt. 'I just
Do it for the mangoes'
Says a notorious Queensland poet, but the
Tone and the squint required
Tell us they've earned the irony. If
You feel you can go to the
Gym and perhaps even
Work out a bit harder than usual
Try and remember the last time
You felt this way. Maybe not so
Long ago. This is what Traherne meant
Surely: that we must treasure
What we have. Monday destroyed itself like it
Had a scratching disease. Tuesday therefore
Lay in a heap. But this is Great
Wednesday like so many others before
  Life is more like a
Pain than a cheese or house, though many
Don't have these properties either. All
This is just talk, however, not an attempt
To define it. Other living things don't
Go around comparing how they

Feel from one day to the next and
Whether they can or can't
Get out of bed, or whether
Not is a choice they have. Is
Human life qualitatively different
From other kinds? Yes, because that's what we
Mean by human: the qualitatively different
From other things. Yet life itself – as a
Definition – is one of the human's favourites
  Neither frogs nor rocks go
To the gym or drink coffee; yet frogs
Feel pain and in some senses
Have things also. Rocks can be said to
Have things too: like orchids or liverworts
They have life. Whether
Rocks are alive or not is not
The issue, but well-being. This
Might be thought of as the
Right amount of life, that allows you
To grasp hold of the
Next swing in the manoeuvre, grabbing someone or
Something and walking
Quickly on as if nothing has
Happened. If a diversion is necessary, try
Cutting open a mango – or
Liberal MP – and waving it near
The other's eyes or nose (if
They have these); alternatively, try reading a poem
Really loudly over and over till they
Get the point. Shall I?

The Letter

Will Cox

Zoe had folded the letter into a dozen different shapes, origamied the hell out of it and unfolded it again, looking for the perfect shape for it to do its work. She thought she should put it in a bottle, maybe, but then decided that might interfere with the natural process, or it might just get wedged between a couple of rocks. Eventually she just screwed the paper up in a ball, making this final, definitive copy of her beautiful letter look like any of the earlier drafts still crowding the bin in her room. She felt a twinge of disappointment that no one would ever be able to read her words. It would be nice to share this feeling with the world, and show people to see that she *could* finish something that she started. *This must be how Emma feels when she finishes a drawing*, she thought.

She sat by the rivulet for a long time, just holding it in the water against the tide, trying to believe in it what she was doing as the dusk set in overhead. The cold air had already made her fingers numb, so it didn't bother her much when the water turned her fingernails blue, and she enjoyed the pressure and flow on her hand.

Inside, she could have put something simple and romantic, like a lock of hair, but she decided she wanted something more solid, a symbol of dedication, something painful to offer the universe, or whatever it was. She'd had her wisdom teeth removed over the summer, and she'd kept one of them in a little plastic specimen jar. Although the marvels of modern medication had spared her a good deal of pain, she still felt that the tooth was a part of her and felt its absence every day when her tongue was drawn to the new hole at the back of her mouth. *I'll feel it*, she thought. *I'll feel the absence it leaves and the new thing it's going to create.*

She'd had a few drinks at home, some of the moonshine from the back of her housemate Richard's wardrobe, so she had a buzz going.

She mustered up all her belief and held the letter in her hands, screwed up in its little ball, tied off with string. *This is it*, she told herself out loud. *This is a turning point, beginning, ending, whatever.* She shut her eyes tight and released it from her hand, into the world. When she opened her eyes, she didn't feel different. The ball of paper was drawn under and under and then thrown up again, and then on downstream, and Zoe felt for the outline of the old orange paperback in her army surplus bag and held it tight to her chest.

Zoe climbed off the rocks and started down the rivulet track, swigging the last of Richard's booze from the hipflask she'd stolen from her Dad before moving out that January. It made her mouth tighten to drink it, but that didn't bother her. She shivered a little beneath the four layers of protection against the cruel valley wind, and tucked her chin into her scarf and walked on. She could feel the letter beside her all the way, could hear her words coursing through the water, through the earth below, could see them glimmering in the water's glow. She could feel the gap at the back of her mouth and the stinging sensation she got when she tongued it.

She followed the track from her magic spot to the party, energised, imagining the words she'd written trickling away and dispersing into the sea, being inhaled deeply into the Earth and exhaled through cracks in the pavement, into backyards, underneath parked cars. She could make this image stay with her only if she didn't look toward the water itself, which would spoil it with the trickling, scummy reality of the bottom end of the rivulet. So she walked with her head high, smiling a secret smile.

When Zoe got to the party, Emma was out the back, already drunk, talking to a boy in a flat army cap with the formative steps towards a beard. They were both laughing: him awkwardly, her raucously, sweeping her heavy fringe out of her eyes.

'Zoe!' Emma called out when she saw her. 'Come and tell Hayden how cold your house is.'

Zoe ran to her, held Emma's hand and nuzzled in to her shoulder. 'Cold,' she said.

'And she lives with a bassoonist –'

'Oboe,' Zoe corrected.

'An Oboe… ist and a Korean science student who's always in the bath,' she laughed drunkenly.

'Sounds like you drew a couple of short straws,' the army cap boy said.

'The uni threw us in together,' Zoe replied.

Emma tilted her empty beer bottle at Zoe questioningly. Zoe shook her head and Emma disappeared into the house.

'I'm Hayden,' said the army cap boy, who was beginning to reveal an irritating tic, a little laugh after every sentence he spoke. 'Are you Emma's friend?'

'Yeah,' she said, but didn't really know where to go from there.

Hayden looked down at Zoe and chuckled nervously. Zoe scoped out the party. The back patio was lit weakly with dusty fairy lights, which were switched on despite there still being plenty of light in the air. Everything had the thick layer of grime and disuse that characterised neglected student housing. There were only about a dozen people, all huddled in groups of three or four. By the grease-encased barbeque was a table with a little laptop on it and several stacked speakers. Hunched over it on a milk-crate was an intense-looking boy, engrossed in the act of playlisting the rest of the night. Every time a song finished and a new one faded in, the boy looked up and observed people's reaction to his selection. When it was inevitably muted, he turned back to his screen.

Emma got back with three beers in hand, and passed one to Zoe. 'Fo' ma bitch,' she said in a faux-New York accent. Zoe took it silently. Emma was three or four further along than Zoe, and halfway down her next beer already. Zoe suddenly felt cripplingly sober.

The third went to Hayden. 'Ah, thanks,' he tittered, and drew a scrappy yellow bag of tobacco from his coat pocket.

'...Hayden does Geography,' Emma was saying. Hayden nodded distractedly, deeply involved in rolling a cigarette. 'And he likes hockey.'

Zoe smiled weakly and said that she studied English, and a confusion ensued in which Hayden thought that Zoe was English, and she had to correct him. He said it was 'totally all right if you are.'

'I'm not,' Zoe said.

Hayden lit his poorly rolled cigarette and passed it on to Emma and tittered some more. A dose of fetid smoke blew in Zoe's face. 'Sorry,' he said.

'It's okay,' she replied. Zoe wanted out of the conversation before it had properly begun. 'I'm just – I'll be back in a minute.' She handed Emma her beer and walked into the house.

Zoe couldn't find the bathroom, not for want of looking. But she found the laundry and realised all she wanted was to stand on her own for a minute. Standing by the door with her back against the wall, she thought of the letter and crossed her fingers tightly.

Emma would thrive out there without her. Zoe was never comfortable in her own skin as she thought Emma must be. She also knew that she could never change what she was, just as years earlier she'd looked in the mirror and realised she'd never look like a film star when she grew up, only an older version of herself.

These thoughts came, and she suppressed them. The letter would change things, she thought.

She went to close the bathroom door but Emma was right behind her, and pushed her way through.

Emma handed the beer, now unappealingly warmed by her hands, back to Zoe, put her hands over Zoe's shoulders and gave her a puppy-dog look. 'Oh, kitten,' she said, and kissed her on the forehead. Zoe didn't meet her eyes. Emma hugged her.

She used to hug, Zoe remembered, and her friends told her she was good at it. She used to open her arms up to them and cling on to them for dear life. It'd been months since she'd seen or even contacted most of them. She didn't hug anymore, and it really didn't bother her. This hug was clunky and a bit awkward. She didn't know where to put her face or her hands, so she just let them fall by her side. And then she did feel like the lost kitten Emma thought she was, helpless and not wanting to be touched.

'This sucks,' Zoe said. 'I thought it would be more…'

'It's not so bad,' Emma said, getting her phone out and reading a text. 'Hugh and that lot are coming in a bit. There'll be more people later, so –'

'I don't know them either,' Zoe said.

'Then know them, get to know them, god.' She was reading her text and smiling to herself. 'Come on, sad kitten' she said, grabbing Zoe's arm. 'Come have another go.'

Not so much later, it was totally dark bar the fairy lights, and Zoe was drunk. Her perception of time blurred. At some point it was midnight, and then one o'clock very shortly afterwards. She felt the words seep from her letter and into the earth below. They warmed her.

Zoe successfully conducted conversations with strangers. That girl was a trainee barista. That'd started a boy, the new owner of a too-expensive coffee machine. He'd boasted until the girl had laughed at him. Zoe smiled at his deep embarrassment.

That boy was from the mainland somewhere, though she'd immediately forgotten exactly where. *One of the boring bits* is how it was filed in her memory. 'What's it like in <*I don't remember*>?' she'd asked him, and laughed. *Chris*, she remembered later. *His name was something like Chris.*

'Oh, not so different,' Chris had said. 'Not so different. Just like, deader, I guess. Yellower-looking. Here's, like, greener.'

Zoe decided she actually liked her new town, and said so. 'I like here.'

He said, 'yeah, well, I didn't get into Sydney, so ...' launching Zoe into her passionate hatred of Sydney and all people from it. People laughed.

She talked to people about nothing, anything. She talked to people about uni.

'I read a book over summer,' said one boy. It was a standard response. 'It was about this guy in Utah,' he started, clearing his throat. 'He was riding his bike across America, and in Utah he got the wheel caught in a ravine. And he fell into this big crack in the rocks, kind of thing, and his bike fell down after him, and wedged his arm into the rock, so he couldn't move it.'

'Did he have to cut his own arm off with a pocket knife or something?' Zoe asked.

'No. But he was stuck there for like six weeks. He had to eat his bike tyres and everything.'

'Oh,' Zoe said, processing this profoundly unsatisfying story. 'So he just got out?'

'Yeah, eventually he managed to move the bike. His arm was all better by the end,' he said, nodding his approval of the happy ending. 'A really inspiring story, anyway. A true story.'

Zoe closed her eyes. She imagined herself stuck, deep inside the Earth, her arm wedged unromantically behind a fallen bicycle, wanting for nothing, slowly dissolving.

Her shoulder bag was still hung across her shoulder. She felt for the outline of the paperback and gripped on to it.

'What's that, a book?' he asked.

Zoe went to move her bag behind her, but the boy forced his hand into her bag and pulled out the skinny orange paperback and turned to the back cover.

'Read it out!' someone said, and Emma buried her head in her hands.

THE LETTER

R.A. Wragby

A Pilcrow Original

'Don't you ever want to rewrite your life, Lady Clarissa? To consign this slavery to the wind, and to be reborn from the Earth?'

This is R.A. Wragby's haunting story of the young girl who married the romantic invalid Lord Raymond, and found herself at grips with a thoroughly unsatisfying marriage.

But when an uncovered secret in the family history throws her into a flirtation with the occult, Lady Clarissa's magical letters envelop the family in flames from which they may never escape.

'A novel of unparalleled suspense from a shrewd moralist... a bright young spark of modern literature.' - SUNDAY TIMES

'That book,' said Emma's voice. Zoe jumped. 'All she ever talks about.' Zoe grabbed the book back from the boy. Emma grinned an overwide grin, all teeth, and handed her a tall glass of something sweet with salt around the rim.

Zoe batted the drink away and groaned. 'I don't want to drink more,' she said.

'Yeah, neither do I. But sure you do,' Emma replied. 'Salt takes the edge off the sweetness,' she passed the sickly-looking drink back, and Zoe took it reluctantly. Emma drank her own.

'I don't...' Zoe tailed off.

If Emma had turned around, she would have noticed that her friend was gone.

Zoe found the bathroom. The walls were a mouldy beige. She latched the door, opened the toilet lid and knelt, legs spread across the floor. She gripped the edge of the toilet bowl with her bare hands. It was her anchor to life. She retched. Nothing came. She tried again. Eventually the retching made the hurt in the pit of her stomach worse. She gave up and rested her head on the warm seat. Zoe noticed there were spots of piss on the floor from the boys' drunken aims and concluded flatly that it was probably now soaked into her tights.

Zoe had only ever been this drunk in the relative comfort of her own flat. When Emma would come over, which was most nights, she'd bring a box of wine or a bottle of something day-glo that they'd mix with lemonade, and they'd drink and listen to music, or Emma would bring her sketch pad and she'd just sit and draw, and Zoe would do her Sudoku or her origami or whatever affectation she'd half-heartedly picked up that month.

Sometimes they'd drink a whole box of white wine between them and then bang on the bathroom door for Ken to get out of the bath when they needed to pee.

Just then, there was a bang at the door and a male voice. Zoe murmured something in response. It seemed to satisfy him, because he didn't knock again, whoever he was.

She knew that Emma would only look for her for a few moments, but that the bathroom would not occur to her, or that she would block out the possibility in case she found her, just Zoe, miserable and sodden on the bathroom floor of the worst house party in town. After what couldn't have been more than a few moments against the toilet seat, she heard Emma's shrill laugh out the bathroom window and resigned herself to doing this on her own.

Emma Forrest blinked as the light behind his head burned into her retina. 'What?' she asked again.

'Your mate,' said the boy Chris.

'Zoe? Zoe-bear?'

'Um… yeah. She looked upset or something.'

'Zoe…' From where she was sitting, and had been sitting for the last quarter of an hour or so, since the world had begun to lurch and pitch, Chris's head wavered in and out of light, making her feel queasy.

'She's… I'll go find her, I think she…' Emma clawed her way out of the canvas deck chair and broke into a run down the driveway.

The street outside was dead quiet, but for the echo of Emma's heavy steps on the concrete. She realised she still had a beer in her hand, took a final swig and threw it into a passing hedge.

The quickest way to Zoe's was the rivulet track, so she crossed the street and headed down someone's driveway. From their backyard, she jumped the fence and landed on the rocks by the narrow stretch of water.

It was colder down there. There was no breeze, just a cool, dew-scented, set-in-the-bones drop in temperature as soon as she got a few feet below road level. The alcohol warmed her sufficiently to take the night in her stride.

Emma crossed the narrow water by the rocks that jutted out, and made her way up the track towards Zoe's flat.

'Emma!' she heard. It took a while to source the cry, but when she did she ran. Beneath the light of the backs of the houses, underneath the overhanging branches, Emma saw Zoe. Sitting on a rock, she thought at first. She began to climb back down to the water. Though gentle, the flow was loud enough to pound in her head.

Closer, she saw that Zoe was fully dressed and waist deep in the water, deeper than Emma had realised the water was. Emma made calm, quiet assurances as she made her way towards her friend. 'It's okay,' she said, 'it's all okay, and we'll just get you out and get you home, and get you dried. Then sleep.'

It was only when she got closer she saw what Zoe was doing, and added up the possibility that she hadn't tripped. Was she reaching for something?

'No,' Zoe said. 'It's okay now.' She was gripping the torn and soggy remnants of some ink-stained paper, which she was flattening out against her chest. Then she opened her tightly gripped fist and showed Emma what looked like a tiny white rock.

'I found it,' Zoe said. 'I got it back.'

Helvetica Poems

Heiko Julien

find me in the club
competing fiercely
for limited resources

* * *

pull up at the club
seeking emotional
gratification from my
desired peer group

* * *

i like to have fun
when it's easy

* * *

fake it til you're fake

* * *

if a child asks their
parents 'why' long
enough the answer
they will eventually
get is 'i don't know'

high school

Emmie Rae

Fuck diamonds. Fuck the rich part of the city. Fuck their dogs. Embrace deeply the roots of us, the 70% water of us. Combine and reject each other. Combine and reject each other. Combine and reject each other. Our nature is truly liquid. There is a deep house in the cave. It is dark and we are nauseous. We don't belong anywhere. We don't know who we are, born to a young mother country, she drank and smoked and fucked our forefathers through pregnancy. We fear pregnancy. We think we can be perfect and we think we matter. We feel anxiety because we care what people think of us. We waste energy being scared when we are predictable. As predictable as water. We are melting. Expanding and contracting beneath the touch of each other. We are slippery fuckers. I don't know what's good or bad anymore. I like when friends are affectionate towards each other. Touch my arms and hug your greetings smack bang into me. People pray to feel alone together, people exercise and think about calories. There is a mountain you can climb if you are not an assassin. Maybe we can keep climbing. Maybe we can keep climbing and never stop. It's the same as down here but the air is fresher. The altitude is higher. Let's get higher and keep getting higher.

Faith Wallah

Samuel Robertson

'India is not Europe.'

It was a truism, of course, but its truth had escaped me. I had previously backpacked through Europe, solo, for twelve months. It didn't seem like a stretch to infer that I'd survive and enjoy India alone, having survived and enjoyed Europe alone. But after I had told my story at great length to Amber, a young hostel owner in Delhi, he repeated the stubborn, salient fact: India is not Europe.

I arrived in Varanasi, the spiritual heartland of Hinduism and the oldest city in the modern world, after a stopover in Bangkok. I retrieved my bag from the carousel, fastened it around my waist and chest, looped my arms through the straps of my small daypack, pressed flush against my chest, and walked through the automatic double doors, into the midday glare, as inconspicuous as a suicide bomber. Outside, a corridor of bodies leaned against steel railings, three deep, each person holding a sign bearing a name. When I reached the pavement by the road, a telephone box of bodies packed in around me.

'Where to, my friend?' asked an elderly tuk-tuk driver, a head shorter than me.

I told him.

'One thousand rupees, good Indian price!' the small Indian man proposed.

'*Arrey*! 950!' said a much taller, much younger man behind him.

The prices continued to inch down as other drivers swarmed, but none dipped below 700 rupees. Then, from somewhere behind the crowd, a voice slipped between the mangrove of legs as deftly as a waist-high child.

'250 rupees—to anywhere in Varanasi.'

There was a rising of voices and flailing of hands as tuk-tuk drivers expressed their indignation at the undercut price; then, almost as suddenly, the crowd settled and dispersed, migrating as a herd towards a couple who had emerged from the automatic double doors.

In the emptied pavement stood the winning bidder. He was elderly, though not stooped by the weight of time; his expression was serious, but not stern. These details, however, came later; my first impression was fully consumed by his hair: a patch-dyed, artificial orange. It looked incongruous against his dark skin.

He brought his hands together in a namaskar. 'What is your good name?'

'Sam,' I answered, returning the gesture.

'My name'—he pressed his left palm flat to his chest—'is Sunil, but you can call me Sunny.'

After shaking hands we stepped off the pavement, crossed the road and turned left, towards the parked tuk-tuks.

'Where in Australia are you from?'

I was impressed that he had guessed my accent correctly. I'd often been mistaken for a New Zealander or Englishman or American.

'Melbourne.'

He considered my response briefly, then moved beyond geography.

'What is your thinking on the Mr. Tony Abbott? Or Tony Rabbit as the Ms. Julia says.'

If a pink elephant stampeded the street at that moment, I could not have been more astounded. Not only did he know the Prime Minister and Shadow Prime Minister of Australia, he understood subtle slights of hand. 'He's not so popular with the younger people,' I explained. 'It's mainly the older, richer crowd.'

'Yes, he is causing the fusses.' He turned sidelong and smiled at me, for no particular reason. His white teeth were brilliant.

'What is it, your thoughts on our President?'

I looked at my feet, shame-faced. I knew nothing of Indian politics.

'Tricky question, it is, because we don't have the presidents! We have the Prime Minister, like your fine country. His name is Pranab Mukherjee. Not such a very good man, if you are asking me.'

I made a mental note to pick up a copy of *India Today* or *Frontline*—two magazines covering political issues that a friend had recommended.

'How do you know so much about Australian politics?'

'I talk it with the peoples, I read it the newspapers.'

'Well, it's very impressive.'

He tried to hide the effect of my compliment by pinching his smile, but it was all the more obvious because of it.

He led me down a line of tuk-tuks: three-wheel vehicles with a green and gold tortoise shell, scooter handlebars and lawnmower engine.

When we arrived at his tuk-tuk I jammed my fat bag in the open air door, then hip and shouldered it through the space and climbed in after it. To the left of the dashboard was an incense stick, burnt almost to the nub, which smelt of cinnamon; centre-perfect, behind the handlebars, was a small, solid figurine of Rati—goddess of love; and to the right of the dash was a sticker with pink, sensuous eyes. It resembled a portable brothel.

Sunny was in the front seat, pulling what looked like an enormous handbrake, to start the engine. When the car rumbled to life he looked at me in the rearview and asked, 'What is the address of your hostel?'

I told him.

'Oh no, sir!' He clapped his hands to his cheeks in a fish-pout.

Turning to face me, he said, 'There are riots at this time, very near your stay. Too very dangerous.'

'What do you mean *riots*?'

'It is taking such a very long time, sir, if I am telling it to your face.'

'Hit me.'

'Sir?' He pronounced it *saar.*

'Tell me, I mean. Why are there riots?'

He explained the story with great animation. Devyani Khobragade, India's consul general in New York, had been arrested on December 12 charged with visa fraud, making false statements, and underpaying her domestic maid, Sangeeta Richard. Indian politicians reacted fiercely to Devyani's arrest, because she had been subject to a strip search. India's indignant reaction involved the removal of all security barricades around the U.S. embassy in Delhi, and a refusal to meet with congressmen. The hullaballoo worked. On January 10th, the day before my arrival in Varanasi, Ms Khobragade was granted full diplomatic immunity and allowed to return to India under that protection. Whilst the Indian government celebrated Devyani's return, there was widespread public anger at the misappropriation of attention. The government had spent enormous resources protecting an accused criminal, but had all but ignored the poor maid, Sangeeta Richard.

From makeshift pulpits and grainy megaphones, students from Varanasi Hindu University protested Devyani's red-carpet treatment by red tape bureaucrats. For them, the case became the face for larger issues: corruption of the rich, exploitation of the poor.

All this anger had been directed in the form of a passionate but peaceful protest, until this morning, when a Muslim student was badly beaten by police after making an obscene gesture. It was a Franz-Ferdinand moment—igniting a chain of events disproportionate to the incident itself. Students took to the streets in protest of both the police brutality and government corruption, resulting in the usual casualties: burning flags, shattered street windows and more than 20 arrests.

'And that, my friendly fellow, is why there can be no going there at this time.'

I felt suddenly exhausted. 'Where the hell *is* safe?'

'When there is a fire in the bush, no one knows which way the wind will blow.'

He reminded me of Rafiki, the crazy-wise baboon from the *Lion King*, who had the same unique mix of youthful exuberance and age-old wisdom.

'Leave Varanasi?' I said, translating his burning bush proverb.

'Only some few days. Wait until the polices have more polices, and students go back to studies.'

It was a less than perfect introduction to India, but I had no desire to walk into a political riot.

I removed my glasses, pinched my nose. 'In that case, I'll go to the train station.'

'Not possible, sir. Trains and buses need to be booked three, four days in advance—ask any Indian. Uncle, uncle!' He waved down a limping man in a white Sari with no shoes. 'He must be booking the buses long time in advance, isn't it so?'

The man ignored the comment with a dismissive hand gesture and walked on. It wasn't clear whether he spoke English.

'You see, not possible.'

'So there's no train, no bus...but I can't stay?'

'Don't worry, my friend. My brother, he have private car.'

Before he'd even quoted the fare, he was on his phone speaking in rapid-fire Hindi. It was loud, fast, animated; it verified Didier Levy's claim that the Indians are indeed the 'Italians of Asia.'

I tapped him on the shoulder. 'How much is this going to cost me?'

'One moment.' He returned to the phone, finished his conversation. 'Five hundred dollars, five days. I take you from Varanasi to Agra, Agra to Fatehpur Sikri, Fatehpur Sikri to Lucknow, and Lucknow back to Varanasi. Very good price.'

I didn't have a local yardstick to measure it against, but back home it cost me $80 for the forty-minute taxi ride from Bayside to Tullamarine—in a taxi that was usually driven by an Indian, I thought.

I decided to commit, then and there. 'Alright,' I agreed. 'How long until your brother arrives with the car?'

'One minute, sir.'

One Indian minute—twenty New York minutes—later, a car parked parallel to Sunil's tuk-tuk.

It was a Suzuki Shitbox. The black paint had vitiligo, with white patches eaten into the paneling. A hubcap was missing from the rear left tyre. The front passenger door was concave.

'Your ride, sir.'

From the steel carnage, the driver appeared. He was Afghan, not Indian; stumpish, not lithe; he was a friend brother, not a blood brother.

'Your driver, sir.'

'I thought *you* were taking me.'

'No, no, no.' He was adamant. 'Raul don't speak the English so good, or the Hindi, but he is most excellent driver.'

'I don't know, Sunny. Five days and he doesn't speak English.'

'This is so good luck, my sir, that you cannot even know it! You two will be playing it, the charades, for days on end. Bollywood will be chasing you! You only need to sing and dance'—and he did exactly that, sing and shimmy, unselfconsciously, in his seat—'and you will be big star.'

I wasn't convinced, and he knew it. His loud exuberance became a quiet calm.

'If you don't have it, the most excellent time, then I will beat Raul with my knuckles, and I will refund you in the fullest.'

He was a political commentator, tuk-tuk driver and salesman.

'Okay.' I committed with renewed vigor. 'Challo!' *Let's go.*

But Raul wasn't ready to go. He smoked a beedie—an Indian-style cigarette, with no filter, made from a rolled green leaf—went to the toilet for so long I can only presume he was constipated, and ate three samosas from a street vendor. My *challo*! was a deflated beach ball, too long in the sun.

Agra was a nine-hour drive. I sat in the back seat, closed my eyes and drifted. Some time later, I was woken abruptly by a loud noise. I jerked forward and ripped my neck. Raul's face was neon-blue, then dipped in darkness, before being lit up again; his hand rested over the horn. He jerked his thumb over his shoulder at a guesthouse with blue lights hung across the awning.

I held my neck as I walked to the reception with my heavy backpack. The room I checked into was small with a thin mattress. I lay down, slowly, mummified between the tight white sheets, and slept.

I woke the next morning feeling disorientated, but the pain in my neck quickly navigated me to the current predicament. After showering I went downstairs and checked my emails. The latest was from Kautilya Society, the hostel I had originally booked in Varanasi. I clicked on it:

> Dear Sam,
>
> We noted that you did not check in yesterday. Please advise if you are still planning to stay with us. Also, please note: if your tuk-tuk driver has claimed that our hostel has shut down, burnt down, or is in some other way unavailable, DO NOT BELIEVE THEM. THIS IS A SCAM. Contact us immediately if this is the case.
>
> Regards,
>
> Kautilya.

I immediately phoned the hostel and spoke to the owner. Sunny's story, as it turned out, was historical fiction—a lie hidden within a fortress of facts. Devyani *had* been arrested, there *had* been an indignant reaction from Indian officials, and there *had* been a protest from the students at Varanasi Hindu University; but the protest had been peaceful, contained to the university grounds, and there had been no danger to anyone.

She advised me to leave Agra for Varanasi by train without telling the driver. The prospect of communicating to Raul, Sunny's burly accomplice, that I had discovered their con and was seeking a full refund, all by way of charades, never entered my thoughts. I followed her logistical instructions to the letter, all the way to Varanasi Central Station, where I arrived 13 hours later.

On the train I had time to reverse-engineer his scam. He had an impressive knowledge of Australian politics, offering the fun fact of Julia's intentional tongue-slip. He then exposed my ignorance by asking if I knew the name of India's President, a trick question I had little hope of answering correctly. His knowledge of Australian politics, and my ignorance of India's, positioned him as the authority. Regardless of where my hostel was, there was a political riot *there*. But more than anything, it was the small details of his story—the full name of each character, the calendar of dates, the specifics of charges—that made me, unconsciously, put my faith in him. I was also jetlagged after an international flight, a *gora* unfamiliar with the local landscape that was at the mercy of a charismatic, conniving charlatan.

But above and beyond the cleverness of his con, there was the baldly factual admission that if I had asked anyone outside his team of two, I would have revealed the scam. I didn't want to wallow on my own stupidity; I focused instead on nailing him to the post.

'A full refund or I'll call the police.'

That was my ultimatum.

'You did not enjoy your trip.' Sunny looked like a rainy afternoon. 'Raul told me that you left.'

'Didn't enjoy my…my…trip? Mate, I didn't enjoy being ripped *blind* by you and the goddam goonda.' I could feel the tendons stiffen in my neck.

'Come, have some chai. We will talk.'

'Mate, I don't wanna *talk*. I want my money. And I wanna get outta here soon as possible.' I was standing in almost the same spot where we had met, at the airport.

'Sit, sit, we will talk.'

'I don't wanna fuckin *sit* or *talk*. I want my *funds*. You understand me? I want my money.' I rubbed my thumb and forefinger together.

'Sit, sit. We will—'

'*Jesus*! I just told ya! I don't wanna *sit* or *stand or anythin*! Are ya *deaf* or somethin! Too much money in ya goddam *ears* or somthin? *Christ*!'

Right then, in front of the lousy stupid cheat, a pair of ridiculous tears climbed up out of my eyes. It was frustration and it was jetlag, and the humiliation of the scam and the jagged pain in my neck. I was fed up to all buggery with the country, the smells and the scams; I just wanted my goddam money.

'I will give you a refund.' His voice was calm. 'But you will need to come with me, to get it.'

Emotional, bewildered, I followed him down an alleyway that smelt of piss and shit and rotting food, into a small shop with techni-colour rugs. There was a girl behind the counter, her pen hovering over a white notepad. She looked up from her desk as we entered. 'My daughter,' Sunny explained, before speaking to her in Hindi. She listened carefully, nodded, rose to her feet.

In the tuk-tuk ride there—wherever *there* was, I had no idea but I was pretty sure I'd end up in a barrel in the bottom of the Ganges—as I knocked knees with his daughter, I wondered if she was part of some new elaborate scam; and when we arrived outside his house and I reluctantly removed my shoes, I wondered if the goonda Raul was waiting for me in the backroom; and when I was forced to have dinner with his family of six, despite a long and passionate protest, I wondered if the chai, cauliflower, sautéed onions or hand-made roti had been spiked; and when all the plates had been cleared, I wondered if dinner was the only compensation I'd receive; and when he dropped me outside my hostel, with all the cash I was owed in my wallet, I wondered why he never said sorry.

RealTree Iced-Tea Lite™

Holly Childs

I like looking at the sun through my eyelashes,
Green ferns, canopy, mossy tuffet,
The colours separate and
Rainbows radiate through palm fronds.
Slide hands across any continent,
Like slime through an hourglass,
That leaf is a miracle,
This fog machine is, like, real,
A dotted line around the edge,
Piña colada vapour pumps through the rainforest,
I go to the Amazon one time,
On Google Street View,
Trek around for hours,
But low-res,
Seems smaller in real life.
Chemtrails
Across the universe,
A crocodile in a suburb after a flood,
Says: Don't drain when it rains,
Carnivorous plants that look like grid-iron masks, or players,
Sludge,
Mud,
Splosh.
The water out of the tap is very thick,
It's hard to drink,

My computer glows light blue,
When it's not switched on,
I'm thirsty,
Satin finish succulents,
Are cacti?
Road Runner on the west coast, bolting away, east,
Water, sparkling,
Running on air
Sprouts,
Foamposites,
Hybrid shells, enoki and moss grow in gaps in the mall,
But then I think I sink down to my waist in mud or sand,
In there,
My see-through time.
I try to transmutate a giant lotus flower into seaweed,
Trying to be
Software that writes its own hard drive,
Destiny,
In the food court,
But I can only breathe out,
Hardware that wants to be free,
Believe.
Like a hardcore girl gets that she will never get up,
Every scene idol is a boy,
Everyone around her says 'no gods, no masters'
They mean it figuratively.
A little girl who lies all the time but everyone believes her, let her sleep!
And an even smaller one who tells her own truth but she's a traitor bitch.
Shut up,

We all wet plants, wet ferns,
Steam spirals,
Wifi fumes,
One final star before your Earth sun rises,
I see you,
Only the cute and the deep will last,
Everything paleo is trending again,
My keyboard shoots,
Fountains,
Hydroponics,
A tablet built for two fingers,
A very girly Venus flytrap,
GM aloe vera,
A time-lapse flower suppurates; you left the light and the camera on too long,
But don't worry; it'll get lots of hits,
It's organic.
Hey, bioluminescence clarifies your hardcore girlfriend's keyboard,
Chemiluminescence glows up all around her mouth and onto her teeth,
She smiles:
Dig up a bone,
A ruin,

The brief life of the love poem

Joan Fleming

The love poem can't get to sleep it keeps thinking about the other
night tossing and burning There are no tired love poems
there are no sad love poems there are no love poems
dreaming by the fireplace or bluffed in the woods What there are, are
wolves! Turn back, little love poem!

The love poem walks all over itself the love poem never listens
there are no listening love poems the love poem betrays its own form
like a ball of bath fizz The love poem lies
It has seven hands thirty–five fingers its gestures are
cinematic and irrational it gets confused when eating peanuts
where is the mouth Oh where is the mouth

The love poem lays itself down in the hotel lobby
the tiles are cold they have been holding the cold close all evening
The skin of the love poem cools and pulses
it has been burning for some time The love poem
lays itself down on the couch it has memories
it does not know how to speak them
aloud it needs help *How are you feeling?*
we ask the love poem The love poem
shuts its eyes There is no cure for the love poem

The love poem gallops ahead with a terrible optimism
its heart is paper and brainwork   More rain
falls in the love poem than can be apprehended
The love poem is never not thirsty   for its own weather

What is your earliest memory, love poem?   Are you afraid
of dark paddocks?   Do you have a totem bird?   I question my love poems'
intentions   I ask them to be quiet while I get on
with my day   I come back to them on my knees
streaming with stinging wish and a crush of the chest   and exaltations
and pinpricked back–stories   I call their mothers in tears
I hang up   I put their mementos out
with the Tuesday trash   I burn their photographs

Sacred Flesh

Alexandra McLachlan

A thousand eyes blinked at once. A short wet shucking noise echoed from eyelids coupled and uncoupled. A knuckle cracked far off into the crowd, it ran through my ears painfully like a clap of thunder. I wanted to scream and pierce the silence, smash it into a pile of sharp dust. They stared at me, sculptures made of shining panes of glass, drained of colour and emotion, I could see through them. They all looked the same, gathered in ritual communion.

Silence erupted and flowed over me, burning my skin. They all shivered, goose bumps along their skin, hands shaking as all those present were named Parkinson. A ringing started to whine in my ears, growing to a loud buzz and eventually a high keen. A fleshy woman wept at the back, loudly, cradling a young boy. She spoke in a foreign tongue but I understood her, I understood every word. I knew her child. I had rescued him from a tar pit and now I would bring him the sun's energy as well as life. That woman knew who I was and knew I was a God.

A tall glistening man walked before me, brandishing a stone knife. To tackle fear I admired the workmanship of the knapper; the stone was smooth and dark as starless night, obsidian. The bone handle was thin and almost pure white. The man spoke in the language of the woman. The crowd started slapping their forearms, chanting a word repetitively. Realisation crept over me, it was made of a radius bone.

A line was organized, the mother and her child at its head. I was bound. He delicately sliced off part of my bicep feeding it to the child in cupped hands.

I was starving.

Notation

David Dick

Then you are left with an idea of yourself
And the feeling of ascending emptiness of the afternoon
'These Lacustrine Cities' John Ashbery

Suddenly calm is replaced by another calm.
It is still and unsettling. A static conclusion,
or a manicured notion, that arrives too quickly
and I am forced to deal with the sentiment,
the double negativity of it all
as if I could find value there
as if I could maybe understand

to stop, slow down and ask you why I feel this way:
not only for us, which is now fortunately beyond question,
but, rather, for myself. How can I
take a step away when you're always waiting
at the fall of the next step? And I'm ok with this.
I want to keep finding you
hidden, which is really just me
in plain sight again, calm, outside some boundary.

Her armchair

Claire Rosslyn Wilson

Cracking like rice fields in heat
shrinking space as they bake,
that was the sound her bones made
when she moved in her chair
trying to make static hours comfortable.
Fat folds pushed against the sides,
a weight that fed on years
and shoved the cushions into deeper dips.

When she died, her bottom hollow
sat alone in the chair
her husband argued with the vacated space.
Her son sat in her body-shape
like he didn't see her there
while he spoke his memories
in idealised settings
and the springs groaned.

Her chair was no longer young,
the faded floral fraying in popular spots
where she'd placed her hands to lean
when making a point,
or repeated cups of unsteady tea
that added brown to pink roses.
But her husband left it in the sun
for company when he watched TV.

sleeptalk

Broede Carmody

sleep leans into
the corners of the room.
a mosquito speaks in tongues,
hovers a hair-length

from your ear.
you swipe it away,
accidentally punch the wall.
I listen to your knuckles as they bruise in the dark.

* * *

afterwards you ask
about my earliest memory.
I mention how I would be washed
in the kitchen sink.

we make love and
it's strange because the whole time I swear
I can smell detergent
on you.

THE *2014 MONASH UNDERGRADUATE PRIZE* FOR CREATIVE WRITING

OVERALL WINNER

Unfruitful

Emily Riches

Sure, they are young, but they have been trying every night for two weeks now. They're both in their twenties, with a new terrace house in the city and an empty room to fill. Well, something is empty anyway. Maybe something less palpable than a room. They both seem to feel it, this emptiness: she isn't sure if it's time, and he isn't sure if it's space, but there's some sort of dimension that's lacking, and so far, they're filling it with sex. Which, really, is neither one nor the other. They don't know this now, but they will learn. For the moment, they still count achievement in material terms. And a baby is an achievement, surely. A way to cement their efforts, a reward for all this trying. When it comes, they will feel so productive. So grown up.

During these grey afternoons they cook packet pasta and sip cask wine under salvaged fairy lights in the courtyard, contemplating the weeds and wild pumpkin vines that curl around the arms of their deckchairs. They listen to the children wailing from the day-care centre on the corner. The walls in these renovated terraces are thin, and they can hear their neighbours murmuring next door, the clink of knives and forks on crockery. They met them briefly by the bins on their first week. Two beautiful young professionals: a heavily pregnant florist and her architect husband, possessing friendly, successful smiles and a hungry eagerness to discuss the passion that united their interests. With articulate enthusiasm, they promoted the ease of urban farming, the convenience of balcony horticulture. Not only are terrace gardens beautiful, functional and sustainable, they make efficient use of space, and are time-saving too. Well.

Inspired, the two of them talk loudly about sectioning off the courtyard's back corner and planting out a little vegie garden. staking a claim on this small terrace. And maybe some tomatoes too. Are tomatoes in season? I guess it doesn't really matter: employing a mantra borrowed student from their student friends, they recited: it's all free food. There's even a pumpkin vine, already established. At the moment its tendrils are bare, but in a few months' time… He also decides he'd like cabbages. They nod to each other and shrug, almost apologetic. It's too easy, really. Too perfect.

She comes home with the soil and seeds the next day, and spends hours digging and gasping and sweating and sowing outside. When she is done, they step back and admire it. They are so proud of their garden. They weed it, they water it. They invite friends over to see it. Soon enough, their kitchen is overflowing with cabbages and carrots, spinach, silver beet and snow peas. They make stir fries, salads, frittatas, and their effusive guests remark on the freshness of the lettuce, the crispness of the legumes. They want to invite their beautiful, functional, efficient neighbours over, but are still embarrassed at their lack of an adequate table and chairs. At the moment, they're sleeping in a nest they've constructed in the middle of the lounge room floor out of pillows and futons. It is here, at the end of each successful visit, that smug drunk sex ensues.

He begins to fill the house with recycled furniture, accumulating odds and ends from garage sales and council clean ups. They toy with the notion of turning the empty room into a study, but neither really needs it: they both decided to defer their university degrees for a taste of real life, and both have yet to find work. The empty room remains undefined. On one return trip from the Salvos, she spies a wooden cot gleaming on the side of the road amid a pile of broken kitchen appliances and cracked crockery. He stops the car. Isn't it beautiful? Isn't it perfect? Surely it will come in handy, particularly the way they've been trying lately. It would hardly take up any unnecessary space either: there's always the spare room. They sit in the car, idling. Isn't this what they've been waiting for, what they've always wanted? Of course it is, of course it is. The cot goes in the boot.

They run into their beautiful neighbours a lot, on their way to and from work. The florist holds her belly in front of her, runs her hands over it. 'Our first,' she says, and the architect beams. The pressure of the excitement is what seems to be swelling her stomach, and they can feel it too, like a sweat, something both internal and external. During these stilted conversations of anxious stretched smiles, they each try to see themselves in the other, but neither quite manages it. Later, a pink ribboned card finds its way into their mailbox, one of their first pieces of mail, an invitation for her to the florist's baby shower: games include guessing the girth, cupcake contests and various consequences for uttering the word 'baby.' She declines the offer, not knowing what to bring.

Weeks pass, and her own stomach stays flat. They talk about visiting the doctor. Offhandedly, not in a 'big deal' kind of way. But because there is no furniture in their terrace to hide behind they speak out of the sides of their mouths. Really, there's nothing to worry about. Haven't other couples been trying for much longer than they have? The neighbours, for example: wasn't it eight months for them? And now look. A beautiful girl on the way, soon to do child-type things, like speaking and breathing and eating dirt at Cabbage Patch Day-Care Centre. Neither mentions the stability of the neighbour's jobs. Instead, they sigh with relief and cuddle into the dank nest of second-hand Salvos blankets, reassured under the faint green glow of the fairy lights. But that night there is no wine, and no sex either.

Once the cot is inside, it looks somewhat shabbier. White paint flakes from it and a few bars are broken. But it is a goal to reach towards. Pressed into the corner it is both too big and too small for the space. The walls expand and contract around it and the carpet crawls away. Is it their imagination, or does the light seem harder and greyer with it in there? Their smiles shrink and grow to hide their disappointment. During their long days at home she wants the door shut, and he wants it open. In both cases, it merely acts as a reminder of what is not there.

The garden, however, is flourishing. Cucumbers and radishes, sweet corn and zucchini sprout without apparent effort. They speculate on why some plants are growing out of season; maybe something to do with the fertility of the soil? The rampant pumpkin vine snakes its way next door, pushing with soft force through cracks in the fence and burrowing, sinuous, beneath foundations. After the last lot of rent cleaned out their bank accounts they haven't got enough money for a TV, so they pass the time watching it grow while eavesdropping on the neighbours. They hear them discussing their labour plans, the emergency bag packed and ready in the car for the fateful hour. Even the walls between them are humming with expectancy.

On the evening the first small body appears in the vegie patch, they think nothing of it. They live close to a day-care, and their fence is quite low. They prop it against the back gate with a scribbled sign: 'Sorry I wandered off! Can I come home now?' Then they giggle and watch from their deck chairs, waiting for an appearance of the bereft, sniffling child and the overstressed yet grateful parent. They wait and wait. As the sun goes down the shadow of the houses fall over them, and without the arrival of either child or parent, they traipse inside, disappointed. They hope it will be gone by tomorrow and earnestly fall into bed, to try and try again. At midnight, as they curl up, spent, on the futon, they hear thudding feet and heavy breathing from the other side of the wall, and a car engine hurtles off into the night. They give each other tight smiles and clutch anxious hands.

By morning, they head into the courtyard to inspect the state of the garden. The journey draws an exclamation: 'The stork has struck again!'

They call the second one their little miracle. Placing it beside the first, they admire the two of them sitting there, stiff brown limbs outstretched, their bunched fists and hard, wrinkled buds of faces. They write another message: 'I missed you, did you miss me too?' They pass the day listening intently, circling one another in the house, unaware that their routes consistently lead them by the back door. 'Oh,' he says, pointing from the window in late in the afternoon. 'Look.' The neighbour's car has returned. Next door is silent and muffled, with a dull, closed-curtain feeling. They think they hear a thin wail through the wall that could be a baby, or just a passing crow.

When the third appears, they suspect their friends of planting them. 'Their idea of a joke,' he says, and she agrees. But the fourth seems more than a coincidence. It's a sign! It has to be. She doesn't say this out loud; just lifts it up and cradles it. 'Kids shouldn't have kids if they keep losing them,' they say together. Laughing, they decide to take the little gathering inside, one in each arm. They cast about for somewhere to put them, and only just hesitate before laying them in the most obvious place. When their visitors spot the small bodies side by side in the cot, they are startled into laughter and suggest the two of them host their own reality TV show. When faced with another empty day they consider this half seriously, lying on their stomachs in the lounge room. They decide to give them names, and mock argue over them, debating the virtues and downsides of Wendell or Adolph, Juanita or Prunella. Sometimes even they don't know if they're joking or not.

By the time the fifth shows up, it is already a game. Now they are waiting. They are expectant. They check the garden together, in the mornings and evenings, crouched and rustling among the leaves. 'Found another,' he cries, lifting its rigid body gently from the savoys. He is particularly satisfied finding them here. Amongst all the vegetables in the garden, these cabbages appeal particularly to him. He is drawn to those leaves, their light, fragile green enclosed in thick, muscular branches of milky-white nerves. They have a sentience to them, he thinks, a secretiveness, as though they have something to tell him. At night, under the fairy lights, they almost seem to glow.

They spend their afternoons picking up the frequencies of children's shrieks floating invisibly from the day-care centre. Yet they still have not seen next door's baby. Nor the florist, or the architect, for some time. The front door remains firmly closed, curtains still and drawn. They strain their ears for a nearby child crying. Sometimes, they hear footsteps, or shards of raised voices, but the words remain unintelligible. One night, she wakes as cramps dig into her lower abdomen, and hears echoes wailing through the house. A chorus of them, desperate and lonely and hungry, so loud she feels it is coming from within her. Struggling to her feet, she stumbles without thinking to the spare room. With every step she pulls against tendrils of warm dank air, curling around her arms and legs, resisting her. She flicks on the light and the wailing stops. She breathes in and out. As the walls shift and tilt groggily, she has the strange sensation she is also standing on the other side of the wall next door, listening to herself breathe. 'Did you hear that?' she says when she crawls back into bed, but he grunts and rolls over, pretending to sleep. His forehead is slick with sweat.

For a reason neither of them can fathom, the vegetables begin to die. They decompose with the same energy they used to grow. Plants brown and curl overnight, leaves wilt, tomatoes rot, leak liquid, as the inner flesh collapses. Cucumbers wither. The zucchinis, when bitten into, fall apart, soft and wet. She can't understand it, and has a wild notion that the pumpkin vine is strangling them all. All except the cabbages, which rustle and creak with robust health. She notices that for this, he is unexpectedly relieved.

The bodies show up at strange rates now: sometimes once a week, sometimes two in one night. This irrational pattern keeps them on edge. When the tenth arrives their laughter becomes slightly forced. Their smiles jerk at the edges and their shoulders tense minutely. As they search, their expectancy takes on a tinge of dread. But as each new body is divulged from the garden, they continue to place them quietly in the spare room. They don't look at each other now, as they stand over the cot and examine their overflowing brood. The room, as a result, has become somewhat denser; foetid and cottony, with a raw, earthy smell. The walls are dry but give the appearance of moisture. Yet neither can bear the thought of throwing their gathering out.

She accuses the lack of windows for the smell, while he decides it is the fault of the furniture. She spends more time outside trying to save the garden, and he assesses the room like an architect in training, moving his hands in theatrical angles that mimic corners and architraves. 'It has to be functional and beautiful,' he says to himself, 'to both conserve time and energy and maximise space.' He slides the cot around, trying different positions, yet at the end of each day he changes his mind and moves it back. She is nervous, hearing the bumps and shoves, his swearing and gasping, from inside. With uncomfortable pangs in her stomach she resists the urge to whisper 'shh.'

It has been weeks since they've seen the neighbours. No cars have arrived outside, no visitors have knocked at the door. They feel guilty about their own lack of neighbourliness, but only become more reclusive. They creep about the house on damp tiptoe. They bring the fairy lights indoors and wind them around the bars of the big, wooden cot. The room retains its warmth and smell of soil, that sterile, vegetable odour, but they stop mentioning it. They don't mention much anymore. Lately, they sleep spine to spine.

She wants to visit the doctor in secret. She knows one of them is unfruitful and she hopes it isn't her. But she never has a chance. The spare room is full now: they lost count at around twenty. After he catches her one evening crying in the bathroom, he slips out in the early morning to kick through the garden and hide the bodies before she wakes up. Today, five more have arrived. He stands contemplating, hands on hips, his innards sinking. Yet, in an instant, a glittering idea arrives, shocking in its utter clarity. Dizzy, he reels. Yes. While brutal, it is their only way out. Feeling both manic and unnaturally calm, he begins what he must do. Inside, he gathers the accumulated bodies into a bundle on their sheet, and tries to lift it, but cannot. He ends up dragging it through the house to the back door. 'Shh,' he implores, feeling watched and illicit. He almost wants to giggle. He takes the shovel and digs, gritting his teeth, spade head biting into the earth, ignoring the endless vibration of wailing voices singing out in distress. Those beautiful bulbous cabbage heads, chopped at the root, go rolling around the courtyard. He digs until he is sweating, until there is space big enough to house the bundle of cloth with its pressing arms and legs. With shaking hands he drops it into the earth and refills the hole, tapping the final mound just as the grey sun crests the houses. She can smell the dirt on him when he comes back to bed and rolls away, clutching her stomach.

They don't eat dinner in the backyard anymore. In fact, they don't really go outside at all. The fairy lights writhe and grow like vines, engulfing first the cot, then the room. They keep the door closed now, for good. They discover that sex isn't time, and isn't space, and it's not even conversation, but now there's none of that either. They stop inviting their friends over for dinner to save money and avoid uncomfortable questions. With nothing else to talk about, they fight over silly things, like doing the dishes and paying rent and their lack of beautiful, functional, efficient things. Those long unfilled and unfulfilling days stretch out ahead of them like empty rooms.

Autumn arrives. Their empty bellies ache. As the pumpkins on the vine begin to swell and ripen, their vegetable patch goes to seed.

THE *2014 MONASH UNDERGRADUATE PRIZE* FOR CREATIVE WRITING

HIGHEST-PLACED MONASH STUDENT

The Wading Pool

Leah McIntosh

The wading pool appeared on a Tuesday.

Sylvia was hanging the laundry when she noticed the small plastic pool sitting in the left corner of her backyard, half-filled with water.

She finished pegging a shirt on the line, the shoulders tight, arms dripping down. Holding a peg in her hand, Sylvia paused, turning it in her palm as she studied this new plastic circle. The wading pool sat ominously poised on the grass, its garish brightness taunting its soft green surroundings. Two gum leaves drifted lazily on the surface, signalling its newness. Sylvia shook her head, dismayed, and turned back to her task. She'd ask Gary about it tonight. She pegged the final garment onto the line and gathering the emptied laundry basket and bucket of pegs, she carried them inside.

* * *

She did not think about the pool until that evening, while they were eating dinner. She remembered when she had a mouthful of steak. Chewing slowly, she swallowed and dabbed her mouth with her napkin.

'Gary, about that wading pool,' she started.

Gary looked up. 'Oh, I found it in the garage.'

'I didn't know we had a wading pool.' She held her knife loosely in her right hand.

'Well, I thought I'd bring it out,' Gary said through a mouthful of meat.

'Don't you think it's a little… ridiculous? For *our* yard?'

'I thought it looked fine. We could paddle in it now and then.'

Sylvia's gaze fell to her plate, 'Well. OK.'

'Glad that's settled.' His cutlery clattered on his empty plate.

Sylvia looked down, carving up more of her steak. 'But… it's just… a pool is a bit… *inappropriate* for April, don't you think?'

But Gary was not there when she looked up. He had cleared his plate and was now in the kitchen, shoving his cutlery into the dishwasher tray.

* * *

On Wednesday, the wading pool seemed larger.

Sylvia was watering her tulips. When she glanced over at the pool it seemed to be taking up at least twice the amount of space it had yesterday.

'Surely not,' she murmured. She walked across the lawn to stand next to the inflated plastic ring. She nudged the pool with her shoe and the plastic trembled, the water sloshing gently against its sides. The leaves shuddered and spun. As if to complement the growth of the pool the leaves had also multiplied since yesterday. Sylvia watched them converge towards the circular sides as the water calmed.

She turned slowly and walked back across the lawn, carefully placing the watering can next to the tap.

* * *

At dinner she mentioned it to Gary: 'Gary… I believe the wading pool has expanded.'

Gary spooned some mash into his mouth: 'Couldn't possibly.' He wiped his lips with the back of his hand.

Sylvia looked up. 'Why so?' She watched as he lined up another spoon of gravy and mash, flecked with peas.

'I blew it up to its full capacity *already*.'

'No… it's larger today. It has… *it's grown*.'

'It's a pool, Sylvia, it's not the bougainvillea, for godsakes.' He shoved the mash in, swallowed. 'Now that – *that* thing's a monster. Every time I bother trimming it – you know what it's like? That monster with two heads that grow every time you chop off one. What's it called?'

'A gorgon? I don't *know*, Gary.'

'No – not a gorgon, they're the ones who turn you to stone. A Hydro?'

'I wouldn't know.'

'Right.'

'I said, I wouldn't know. That doesn't sound right, though.' She looked down, placing her fork and knife on her plate.

'I'm just sick of trimming that damn thing.' He picked up his glass, taking a gulp.

Sylvia looked at him evenly. 'I wish you would remove the pool from the yard.'

'Fine.' His glass hit the table. 'I'll empty it after dinner.'

'Thank you.' Picking up her plate and glass, she left.

* * *

Standing on the porch on Thursday afternoon, Sylvia looked out into the yard to find that the swimming pool had somehow replaced her lawn. She stepped off the porch. When she reached the pool, she crouched, water lapping at the sides. She skimmed her fingers across its surface. The tiles of the pool, also blue, seemed endless; she could not pinpoint a bottom, merely an infinite stretch.

She wondered if she should mention it to Gary.

Turning back and walking into the house, she found herself glancing at it through the kitchen window.

* * *

Gary called, late in the afternoon.

'A business meeting has come up – I will be in Sydney for the next few days.'

Sylvia found herself nodding, and then realised he could not see her. 'Okay. Yes.' She paused, glancing out the window. 'Do you need anything from home?'

'I should be fine. I'll see you on Sunday.' He hung up.

Leaning against the kitchen bench to eat her dinner, she looked out at the pool as she chewed.

* * *

On Friday, Sylvia was afraid to look into her backyard, so she spent the day inside. She read, she organised her paperwork. She refused to open the kitchen curtains. She refused to look at the kitchen curtains. She refused to even consider the kitchen curtains. They were cream and didn't quite meet in the middle and they left a small gap through which she could see a sliver of foamy blue. She ate at the dinner table, alone, and left the dishes on the kitchen bench, and when she retired to bed she refused to listen to the waves pounding softly against her porch.

* * *

On Saturday, Sylvia woke to a faintly tangy smell permeating the house. It clung to her as she followed it, passing slowly through the hallways of the house and finding herself at the back door.

She flipped the latch, swinging the door open. The scent intensified. She had opened her door to an ocean that lapped at the fences of the yard. The balcony, filled with sand and dotted with a few shells, beckoned her to sit.

Sylvia sat.

The sea softly swept to and fro, white froth barely forming. At the far-left corner of her backyard, she could see water swilling around her eucalyptus tree, hanging high above the house. The swing they had attached to one of the stronger branches hung low above the water. Her tulips, submerged, swayed merrily against the fence. Soon the water was kissing her feet, the tide coming in.

She wondered what would happen to her tulips.

When she sat, watching the sea sway and recede, a strange emptiness invaded her chest. It sat there gently; as if, perhaps, it had always sat there, a part of her body like a lung or a liver. But like lungs and like livers, Sylvia had remained unaware of it until it presented itself to her. As she drifted off to sleep that night, she imagined two hands pushing into it, this dark cavity, searching for a wall, a bottom, an end.

* * *

On Sunday, Sylvia woke up to a blue sky. She walked to her wardrobe and, digging through a drawer she found her swimsuit. The swimsuit itself was white with light blue streaks, an inversion of the sky. She pulled it on. The synthetic material rolled up from her legs, and stretched out across her stomach, a second skin.

She walked downstairs, out the backdoor, past the sand. She stared down at the water. She bent her knees and bringing her chest down to meet them, she stretched out her arms above her head. She pushed forward with her legs and dove neatly into the water.

* * *

Gary stepped out of the cab, shutting the door behind him. Holding his briefcase, his duffle bag thrown over his shoulder, he walked up the path, stopping at the door to pull out his key. Once inside he poured himself a glass of water and looked out the kitchen window. Sylvia was lying on the grass, still.

'Sylvia?' he called. 'What are you doing? I'm home.'

Her dress, white with light blue streaks, was rippled around her.

'Sylvia?'

It was a winter dusk that spread over the lawn: deep blue, under a darkening sky.

'Sylvia!'

He swung open the back door, and stepped out onto the porch. He slipped slightly. Righting himself, he bent down to inspect the slippery substance between the wooden slats and his shoe. He rolled the granules between his fingers. He paused.

'Syl?'

* * *

Sylvia floated through her garden, brushing the tulips with her fingertips, swimming amongst the gum trees and bougainvillea. She let the water flood past her, through her, into the newfound cavity, watery fingers reaching into the darkness, filling the space. Her lungs, bursting, reminded her of their existence. She swam on, looking for the bottom, diving further down.

She listened to the water flood past her and tried to make out whether it was whispering to her or if she could hear Gary's voice faintly calling her name.

She closed her eyes, she stretched out her arms.

Sylvia swam on.

Chorus

Anders Villani

a bunch of boys and girls in a tree
hollow – probably a wombat's home
before the city rose and left green islands –
are blowing waxy leaves, like apple skin.
I know the exact sensations they're having.
they tell me not to see them, so I don't.

the way it works is a man on the footbridge
with planks missing plays his harmonica,
crimson rosellas at their evening
conclave in that same decimated elm
all squawk crazy, then girls and boys blow
like a leaf chorus for the birds and the man.

ahead, the MCG light towers come into view.
by the looks of it, they're nearly at full power
for tonight's cross-town rival clash –
gulls are already marshaled on the roof
ready to forage for worms on the ground behind
play, eat whatever alms get winged their way.

I find I am mixing up my part in the harmony
we used to hum on leaves during recess with
my schoolyard girlfriend's, who could wolf-
whistle with her hands and was the loudest.

in fact, I don't think I ever figured out how
to turn a leaf into music. I just mimed well

and I loved her. on my lunch break in Flagstaff
Gardens this afternoon, some disturbance in
the Friday waveform was noted – businesspeople
circling near the lawn bowl greens – cries,
a chill ripple. I parlayed my half-eaten sandwich
to the possums for a dog's bashed-in corpse.

boys and girls with tiger and hawk
merchandise stream from inbound trains.
trumpets, harmonicas, keg-drums, the man
who heads one of the cheer squad sections
I know from the TV. suddenly I consider
buying a ticket, or moonlighting records,

anything for admittance, I want to scream out
my lungs every goal and contentious tackle,
I want to sing the rites of 'Melbourne's religion,'
mob an all-night pub with the rest of the flock,
eat a burger as the first red spatters of morning
look more like blood than blood. stroll into work.

but the rule with undertows is never struggle
against them, struggling does nothing
but wreck your chances, render you powerless
to swim back once the danger
self-destructs and the shore is a misted flat line
so I throw my loose change down. it chimes

down the chute. a blue ticket comes out,
the hand that pulls it free is trembling.
clownish number games, numbers of bodies
trying to fit in the tree hollow with leaves
to play, play on my mind at my station.
I mime the exact motion, the exact

sensation of being all of them at once,
scarcely with room to raise their hands
and put the instruments to their lips,
and I pass through the turnstiles humming,
the hum trickles through my throat like oil,
and I buy some beers, ready for the big game.

What Comes After Hope

Manuel Atreu Abreu

Jonathan Franzen age 7, getting a lollipop from his doctor. Jonathan Franzen age 7, eating swedish meatballs or something. Jonathan Franzen age 10, re-reading the Narnia books every month. Jonathan Franzen as a tween afraid of his first erection. Jonathan Franzen as a tween getting his first pair of glasses. Jonathan Franzen age 15, popping pimples in a mirror for 2 hours. Jonathan Franzen age 15, wondering if anyone will ever want to touch him. Jonathan Franzen age 15, getting the mail for his mom. Jonathan Franzen age 17, wondering if he could pull off a peacoat. Jonathan Franzen age 18, encouraging people to call him 'the Franz.' Jonathan Franzen age 19, losing his virginity and crying. Jonathan Franzen age 20, meeting Michael Martone. Jonathan Franzen in his 20s, getting lost in Munich. Jonathan Franzen in his 20s, aware of his chronic low-grade depression. Jonathan Franzen age 23, getting married in rueful sunset. Jonathan Franzen age 25, pretending to have read *Moby-Dick* in conversation. Jonathan Franzen age 32, re-reading *The Great Gatsby* for the 6th time. Jonathan Franzen age 35, buying irish spring soap at cvs. Jonathan Franzen age 40, subsisting almost entirely on sadness. Jonathan Franzen age 40 on 81st and Madison debating smoking a cigarette. Jonathan Franzen age 51, saying 'you have to love before you can be relentless.' Jonathan Franzen age 51, getting his glasses stolen and ransomed for $100,000.

Hibernating is one and breathing is another

Emilia Batchelor

On the subway to the mountain women jostled together in day glo hiking outfits and holographic visors. The visors had glittery decals on them, and they had dust masks over their faces. The carriage looked like the Ikea ball pit on mushrooms. No one seemed to notice me though I felt very different to them all and none of our thoughts could ever be common. I would follow the lights cast by their outfits up the track we'd hike.

I had been feeling stressed.

I'd been worrying about regressing mentally, becoming a big baby with a bed and a Barbie kitchen in my playpen flat. A dark toilet and no one to talk to. In the supermarket I had felt anxious about the way my pants gripped my calves but not the rest of my legs it felt that uncomfortable. I was anxious about lots of things being at my eye level rather than above me and my field of vision being crowded. I frequently worried about losing all my memories one morning.

When I felt weird like that, I walked.

At the train station I walked in on one woman in a cubicle in the toilets. She didn't make any kind of protest when I slowly opened the door, but then I saw her feet and quietly closed it again. Her feet were so small I almost missed them. The old lady next to her was having a hard time and there were urinating sounds and then farting noises. She was loudly puffing and moaning a little as she put more effort into things.

Ah, these were the sounds of hard work, and they were encouraging.

The first woman came out. She looked at my face with kind of tired interest. Big, white and young. I looked at her face with interest. Old and very clear. It gave the impression her eyes were much bigger behind the skin folded around them. I was much taller than her, and her thinning hair displayed admissible evidence that buildings crumbling from the top and fall down, and rocks break off cliffs and fall, and snow melts and runs down the mountain, gathering speed.

The topography was rapidly changing everywhere, and it felt risky.

The floor was wet with fresh cleaning water. The toilets were mostly white or silver or covered with a leafy green decal. I hovered above the toilet seat while pissing. A small burn began in my thighs. An old woman sweeping under the door while I sat in a cubicle had a broom made from rubber. I grinned my usual grin when showering or in toilet spaces imagining coming out somewhere entirely different, and here somewhere else would be heaven.

The ladies bath and sauna section of heaven of a million breasts swollen with the glory of god.

I could hear the woman next door straining still and I could hear her straining when I washed my hands and again when I left. The escalators at the train station were covered in the decal leaves. The station was the size of a museum. Outside a black and blue bird made sounds from a nearby post and it sounded like the woman straining.

There were the women, covered in glitter, masks, decals at the base of the track. There were many birds. There was a droning sound and a jackhammer in the distance. The trees were mostly dead from winter. A monk was singing and beating a drum next to someone selling water and rice wine and playing loud pop music.

A boy swung around on the path and his face was suddenly extremely close to mine. He turned back around the right way. The lasting impression his face gave was of mental disability. Him and a girl were loudly playing at imaginary phone calls, saying Hello? Who is this? And then a name, and laughing hysterically. Laughing hysterically but not dropping pace. Everyone up and up mountain. Felt like running and jumping on one of their backs and hollering.

I was getting hot and my legs began to hurt. My jumper was prickling inwards.

A Maltese terrier in a sportwear jacket went past me. His owner had a baseball cap that said Tank. The dogs little ball sack bounced back and forth like a bell just underneath its tail at the intersection of its two hind legs. It was the colour of rotten banana skin with long white wisps of hair. Its breath sounded like velcro sticking and coming unstuck over again. I could hear something tinkling from its collar, a little bell.

The jackhammer, the man adjusting the radio at his waist to drown out Shakira, some lanterns bobbing in the breeze, kept me thinking about those tiny, delicate balls. I tripped and bounced up a little.

Tinkles, the sounds of a little dog straining. Rapid readjustments of images at a certain level.

I noticed the ends of the trees had green shoots peeking out of them.

There were signs of sexual activity everywhere, and a mountain was a sponge that absorbed and reproduced smells and images inside me.

Thinking I will jump on you, you had better keep the pace, in a large radial directive to everything around me, and it was encouraging.

At the top of the mountain, you could kind of see the city through the haze. It was too polluted to feel cold or see clearly. Even the colors looked like they were struggling in the atmosphere. Lots more panting. I couldn't hear my own breath as if it had taken a different path and gotten lost.

A large group of women unstrapped themselves from poles and removed their boots. They lay down mats and on the mats they removed food from Tupperware and packages in alfoil. Chopsticks pecked at everything. They formed a circle and talked rapidly toward a central space. The central space was a net that filled with everyone's thoughts to become a community of impulse and experience.

How I wanted to dive into that space and be absorbed and released.

It was pretty exciting. It occurred that everyone was getting a little drunk.

The women packed up and put things in garbage bags into their bags. Their eyes were tired and cloudy with rice wine. It seemed like a long way down to the cubicles after having come all the way up to consume the spread. It seemed meaningless but also we were having very dissimilar thought processes.

Like it seemed like an idea to me to wander off the path and lie down with leaves large enough to cover your face and body, that seemed exciting.

At the bottom of the mountain in the dying light it was blackish.

I sat with some woman on a round marble stone at the base, facing out and on our phones. My hands felt very cold, inhuman object like. One lady hummed with the monk. Her friends were quiet just on their phones.

On the subway, I was thinking about the blood-sucking deer with antlers that might live near the DMZ but I wasn't sure. A man was taking two by two steps in a square while holding the handholds suspended from the ceiling. He had his eyes closed and was breathing at a quarter speed rhythm with his steps. He seemed weary enough to slip if he let go. Then he would hiccup and it would all be back on.

I promised if he did fall I would grab the handholds, close my eyes and take up for however long necessary, and that seemed peaceful.

Moreira

Bella Li

In his diary he spoke of the existence of internal deserts.

(Butlin)

And when the image speaks, it is also a kind of ruin. The blank paper receding as a loosed bullet to the gun—though time is neither lead nor waiting. "A few days ago, I discovered the photography of Carlos Moreira." The name recalled to me a man I had once met, while staying at a Jesuit mission in the north of São Paulo. The year was   . I had travelled to the mission to gain respite from an unbearable grief. My companion and I stood on a vast plateau, which stretched for miles in all directions (the coast to our right and our arrival: "After a perilous journey and a shipwreck"). Twelve thousand fish drying on the floodplains, the colour of milk. We had embarked, after a perilous journey—and our hope so dwindled, the sea so blue, the plateau stretching in all directions—when, over the horizon, the first of their number appeared. Closer, we saw that they were not men but birds, exceedingly beautiful. We inquired as to the role of the sorcerers in their midst. And they answered, "Father, the gold is in Minas Gerais." What follows is a series of indecipherable [*Auto: Cartas, Informações, Fragmentos Históricos e Sermões*], but in due course we descended to the coast (twelve thousand on the floodplains, the colour of milk). Years later, I awoke to find—Moreira (*todo*), Moreira (*nada*)—the taste of the sea in my mouth. The coast to the right. And beneath me the gold plateau: vast desert of the soul, the sea receding. "In the immense wilderness."

THE *2014 MONASH UNDERGRADUATE PRIZE* FOR CREATIVE WRITING

Judges' Report

Felix Nobis, Robert Watkins and Meg Mundell

Writing often feels like a lonesome and uncertain pursuit, with opportunities for validation coming few and far between. Prizes are a step toward redressing this: they reward writing talent, effort and skill with public recognition, publication and—if you're lucky—cash. They also offer something less tangible, but perhaps more valuable: encouragement.

Now in its third year, the Monash University Undergraduate Prize for Creative Writing delivers on all these fronts. It's an unusually inclusive prize, welcoming short fiction, non-fiction narratives and narrative verse. This year, for the first time, entry was open to both Australian and New Zealand university students, enrolled in either an undergraduate or honours degree. The shortlisted authors have had their names spotlighted, their writing skills affirmed. The winner, or winners in this case, will be published in *Verge*, Monash University's creative writing journal, and will share one of Australia's richest accolades for short creative works: a prize pool of $5000.

This year's shortlist offered rich pickings, too, for the judging panel, and we'd like to congratulate the shortlisted authors for their efforts in crafting these impressive pieces. There was some wonderfully strong writing, and some mature and assured voices. We met a range of memorable characters—from inner-city hipsters to clairvoyants, from backpackers to runaways, elderly widowers to university students; and encountered an evocative array of settings, all convincingly crafted—from urban backyards to strip joints, from the Australian outback to beaches, from bathrooms and vehicle interiors to mythical forests and freezing campsites.

The shortlisted works ranged from realist to experimental in style, and covered both fiction and non-fiction. Many included allegorical elements, and in most cases this worked in their favour, lending the piece a satisfying structure. If we had a reservation, it was a general one: in a competition that invited a wide range of forms, it was a little disappointing not to see a greater number of alternative forms, such as non-fiction, monologues or poetic narratives, amongst the wider field of entries.

This year's winning entries were both fictional works. In different ways each explores relationships, and combines high-level writing skills with a firm grasp of the short story form. While both stories—purely by coincidence—share the setting of a domestic backyard, neither takes a realist approach. Importantly, these two writers have clearly polished their work, re-drafting, editing and proof-reading until none of the cracks showed: they've invested that particular kind of effort that, paradoxically, makes a piece feel effortless.

Good short fiction is a bit like charisma: tricky to pin down, but you know it when you see it. For Will Self, a short story is 'a shard, a sliver, a vignette'; for Lorrie Moore, if a novel is a film, 'a short story is a photograph'. Neil Gaiman describes short stories as 'tiny windows into other worlds and other minds and other dreams'; for Paolo Bacigalup, they are 'hand grenades of ideas'. All these metaphors could apply to our winning entries.

The first prize of $4000 goes to *Unfruitful*, by Emily Riches, from the University of New South Wales. In a collection of works unafraid to explore the profound within the everyday, this beautifully melancholy story was a highlight. The compact, well-crafted narrative shows a mature understanding of how a short story should be shaped. There is an assuredness to the writing that allows the reader to surrender to this world, and a restraint that allows us to invest in the story—an investment that is rewarded at every turn. A backyard vegie garden offers the perfect lens through which to explore the fertility and infertility of life. Adroitly handled, and balancing the mystical with the mundane, this work makes the most of what the short story form has to offer.

The Highest-Placed Monash University Student Prize of $1000 goes to *The Wading Pool*, by Leah McIntosh. Through twelve scenes occurring over six days, this short story skilfully depicts a process of transformation. Whether in her backyard or within herself, a woman learns to accept and ultimately embrace an initially unwelcome change. Controlled and original, this is an ambitious and clever work that explores themes of alienation, escape and metamorphosis. It remains fresh over several readings, a testament to the author's command of the words.

Judging this year's Monash Prize has been a pleasure. We look forward to reading more work from the winners and shortlisted authors as their writing careers progress.

Contributors

Editors

Gabriel García Ochoa grew up in Mexico City and has been living in Australia for the last ten years. He is coursing the final semester of his PhD in Creative Writing at Monash University, where he has taught Postmodern and World Literature, Translation, and Spanish and Latin American Studies. In 2013 he attended Yale University's Writers' Workshop and the Institute for World Literature at Harvard University. His first novel, *The Blue Book*, will be published next year.

Rebecca Jones is a career journalist across print, television and radio. She has worked for the Australian Associated Press and Bloomberg News in Australia, throughout Southeast Asia and in New York. She holds a Master of Arts in Writing from Swinburne University and is currently completing a PhD in Creative Writing at Monash University investigating a 150 year old cold-case as a vehicle to examine new ways of writing about the inner lives of historical people.

Oscar Schwartz is a poet and blogger from Melbourne, Australia, currently writing a PhD investigating whether computers can write poetry. Oscar has been published in *The Best of Australian Poems (2013)*, *The Lifted Brow*, *VICE* and *The Age*. He tweets regularly from @scarschwartz, and blogs from botpoet.tumblr.com.

Authors

Manuel Arturo Abreu is a poet and artist based in Portland and New York City. They are building coping mechanisms of precarious thriving. Read more of their work at twigtech.tumblr.com and @Deezius.

Emilia Batchelor is 23 and living in Seoul, Korea. Originally from Sydney, she co- runs *God Ate My Google Drive*. She tweets from @bemiliamilia.

Coral Bracho was born in Mexico City in 1951. She is the recipient of the Aguacalientes National Poetry Prize (1981), and a Guggenheim fellowship (2000). She has written six books of poems, including *Peces de piel fugaz*, *Tierra de entraña ardiente*, and *Firefly Under the Tongue*.

Broede Carmody is 21-years-old and a poetry editor for *Voiceworks* magazine. His poetry has appeared in *Cordite*, *Voiceworks*, *Visible Ink*, *Verge* and elsewhere. He likes chai more than you do.

Holly Childs makes work around digital semiotics, transformations of language and culture, aberration, fashion. Her debut novella *No Limit* was released by Hologram in April 2014.

Will Cox is a writer from Melbourne. His non-fiction has been published in *The Big Issue*, *Broadsheet* and *Catalyst* and his fiction has mostly been confined to the inside of his brain. He is currently finishing a writing and editing degree at RMIT and is launching a small press publisher Casuals Network Press later this year.

Peter Dawncy lives in the Dandenong Ranges east of Melbourne. He has a Bachelor of Arts with majors in English and Philosophy from Monash University and is currently completing his Creative Writing PhD. Peter won the 2010 Monash Prize for Poetry and has had fiction and poetry published in various Australian journals and magazines.

David Dick is a Melbourne poet and a PhD student at Monash University . He has had poetry published in the online magazine, *otoliths*.

Killian Donohoe was born in Dublin, raised in Melbourne, and has just finished an Arts/Law degree at Monash University.

Anne Elvey's first full length poetry collection *Kin* was published by 5 Islands Press in April 2014. Anne is managing editor of *Plumwood Mountain: An Australian Journal of Ecopoetry and Ecopoetics*. She lives in Melbourne, Australia, and holds honorary appointments at Monash University and University of Divinity. anneelvey.wordpress.com.

Michael Farrell was born in Bombala, NSW. He has a PhD on Australian colonial poetics from the University of Melbourne. Recent publications include *the thorn with the boy in its side* (Oystercatcher); *same! same! same! same!* (sus); *enjambment sisters present* (Black Rider) and *open sesame* (Giramondo). He lives in Fitzroy.

JOAN FLEMING Joan Flemming is New Zealand writer living in Australia and studying towards a PhD in ethnopoetics at Monash University, Melbourne. Her writing has appeared in *Sport, Landfall, Hue & Cry, Turbine, Snorkel* and *Minarets*. She is currently working on her second book, a collection of failed love poems.

MIRA GONZALEZ is the author of *I Will Never Be Beautiful Enough to Make Us Beautiful Together* (Sorry House, 2013). She is from Los Angeles, California.

STU HATTON is a poet, freelance writer and editor. He also works in mental health research at the University of Melbourne. His books are available from http://www.lulu.com/spotlight/stuhatton. Sometimes he posts things at http://outerblog.tumblr.com.

HEIKO JULIEN is a writer from the Internet. In 2013, he published *I Am Ready to Die a Violent Death*. In 2014, he wondered if this title would be cause for mean-spirited joking were he to actually die. He hopes not.

BELLA LI is an editor, PhD candidate and a managing co-editor at Five Islands Press. Her poems have been published in a variety of journals, and anthologised in *Best Australian Poems* (Black Inc, 2012 and 2013) and *Contemporary Asian Australian Poets* (Puncher & Wattmann, 2013). Her chapbook *Maps, Cargo* (2013) is published by Vagabond Press.

LEAH MCINTOSH is completing her English honours at Monash University. Most of her life may be summarised in a line lifted from David Foster Wallace's *Infinite Jest*: 'I do things like get in a taxi and say, "The library, and step on it."'

ALEXANDRA MCLACHLAN is a nineteen-year-old Bachelor of Arts student at the University of Queensland. She started writing as a small time hobby a few years ago and it has now consumed her focus. She hopes to go on to complete a master's degree and if it all works out, publish a book or two.

NICHOLAS MODRZEWSKI is a painter and writer and works for a philanthropy consultancy called Philanthropy Squared.

EMMIE RAE is a writer from Sydney and co-founder of digital / irl spoken word night, God Ate My Google Drive. @emmieeerae.

Emily Riches is a writer from Sydney and the winner of the 2014 Monash University Undergraduate Prize for Creative Writing. She is currently immersed in an English and Art Theory degree at the University of New South Wales. Emily's work will be appearing in *The World To Come*, anthology published by Spineless Wonders later this year.

Sam Robertson was an assistant editor for *Verge* in 2010 and has been a contributing writer in previous editions. He recently graduated from Monash University with an Arts/Commerce degree and now spends 9-5 as a qualitative market researcher learning 'projective techniques'. His recent trip to India was a mixed experience.

Marika Sosnowski graduated from Monash University with a Bachelor of Laws and First Class Honours in International Politics. She has taught Middle East politics at Monash, Melbourne and La Trobe Universities and worked at the Jewish Museum of Australia. She is currently an international development consultant focusing on Syria.

John Tranter is an Australian poet, publisher and editor. He has published more than twenty books of poetry, and founded the internet quarterly literary magazine *Jacket* which he published and edited until 2010. His most recent volume, *Starlight: 150 Poems*, won the 2011 *Age* Poetry Book of the Year.

Anders Villani was born in Melbourne. In 2013, his poetry appeared in *Award Winning Australian Writing*, and his fiction was shortlisted for the Lord Mayor's Creative Writing Awards. Anders is currently an MFA candidate in poetry at the University of Michigan, Ann Arbor. He is also a two-time recipient of the John Marsden Prize for Young Australian Writers.

John Williamson is an English poet living in Chicago and teaching at the University of Chicago following a career in mental health services in the UK. He has published six collections of poetry with Salt and a collection of critical essays, mainly on recent British poetry. His most recent book of poetry is *Reckitt's Blue* from Seagull Books.

Claire Rosslyn Wilson is a freelance arts practitioner in the areas of nonfiction and poetry, with experience as a writer, arts administrator and researcher across the Asia-Pacific region. She has a strong commitment to investigating cross-cultural exchanges and how creative processes can explore themes of movement and migration. You can read more about her here: clairerosslynwilson.com.

Acknowledgments

This tenth edition of *Verge* would not have been possible without the help, support, and guidance of many people. We would like to thank Dr. John Hawke who was our mentor throughout this editorial process. We are also very grateful to the newly minted School of Languages, Literatures, Cultures and Linguistics for their financial support. Thank you Melinda Harvey and Jodie Wood for your help with PR and general administration. To the staff of Monash University Publishing, our warmest thanks, in particular to Nathan Hollier and Kate Hatch for their patient guidance through what were for us hitherto unchartered waters. We also wish to thank Sam Twyford-Moore, Director of the Emerging Writers' Festival, for the new association that was established this year between *Verge* and the EWF; working with you was a great pleasure. Thanks are also due to David Abraham Michael, who illustrated the remarkable front cover of this anthology. Finally, we are very grateful to each of our contributors—the exquisite bricks and mortar of this book—and to our anonymous referees for their insight and generosity with their time.

Gabriel García Ochoa, Rebecca Jones, Oscar Schwartz